Endorsements

"This wonderful little book is a series of letters to Steve Lawrence's three sons. Each letter, focussing on a particular virtue, is full of traditional wisdom drawing on Scripture, the writings of the saints, and personal experience. Beautifully written and deeply personal, these letters underscore the importance of aiming for greatness as a man – so very needed today when authentic masculinity is so often misunderstood and sidelined. Highly recommended!"

Paul Morrissey
President, Campion College, Australia.

"Tiny Book for Giant Men" is anything but tiny!

It is written by a big man and some of the characters in the narrative are big men.

There is nothing that I can find like this! Anywhere.

Stephen unapologetically writes to his three sons (Dom, Jerome, and Ambrose) about the characteristics of what it takes to be a giant man.

He outlines how they could be great men, how they could be GIANTS if they embraced the 19 essential qualities of manhood.

In an age of information overload, there is very little written about how to be a great Father and a great man. There is a social crisis in manhood. So when I received this script for review and read these challenging and informative 19 chapters, I cheered out loud!!

This book is small in size, there are only 100 pages. However, it is Huge! Every boy on the journey to manhood, and every father, needs to jump in and read this book. This is a road map, a handbook, and an instruction manual for great manhood. A book from a giant of a man, for Giant Men.

Robert Falzon
Author of "The Father Factor" and "Raising Fathers."

"An awesome book! The Tiny Book for Giant Men is a welcome voice in the building crescendo of contributions furthering Catholic male spirituality, offering a refreshingly personal and honest presentation of what it means to be a man of God. Steve Lawrence wonderfully balances Sacred Scripture with practical, real world advice that speaks clearly and directly, challenging men to live their faith with courage and conviction. This book is an invaluable resource for all Catholics who care about the intellectual, physical, and spiritual development of the next generation of men."

Deacon Harold Burke-Sivers
Author of "Building a Civilization of Love:
A Catholic Response to Racism."

"The Catholic Men's Leadership Alliance operates from a simple motto: Strengthen the man, strengthen the family. Strengthen the family, strengthen the Church. Strengthen the Church, transform the culture. Steve Lawrence provides a great guide to make this a reality in his Tiny Book for Giant Men. If you want to be strengthened as a husband, father, son, brother, and - most importantly - as an apprentice of Jesus, you need to read this book."

Dan Donaldson
Vice President,
Catholic Men's Leadership Alliance

Steve Lawrence

The Tiny Book for Giant Men

© Steve Lawrence 2023

All rights reserved. Except for quotations, no part of this book may be reproduced or transmitted in any form or by any means, electronic or mechanical, including photocopying, recording, uploading to the internet, or by any information storage and retrieval system, without written permission from the publisher.

Published by Parousia Media Pty Ltd
PO Box 59 Galston, New South Wales, 2159
+61 2 8776 8778
www.parousiamedia.com

Cover design: Jerome Lawrence

ISBN: 978-1-923131-24-8

Printed in Australia

Table of Contents

Dedication．．．．．．．．．．．．．．．．．．．．．．．．．．．．．．．．．．．．7
Foreword．．．．．．．．．．．．．．．．．．．．．．．．．．．．．．．．．．．．．11
1. Freedom．．．．．．．．．．．．．．．．．．．．．．．．．．．．．．．．．．．．13
2. Purpose．．．．．．．．．．．．．．．．．．．．．．．．．．．．．．．．．．．．．17
3. Being and Recreation．．．．．．．．．．．．．．．．．．．．．．．．21
4. Silence．．．．．．．．．．．．．．．．．．．．．．．．．．．．．．．．．．．．．．25
5. Guardian．．．．．．．．．．．．．．．．．．．．．．．．．．．．．．．．．．．．29
6. Presence．．．．．．．．．．．．．．．．．．．．．．．．．．．．．．．．．．．．．33
7. Courage．．．．．．．．．．．．．．．．．．．．．．．．．．．．．．．．．．．．．37
8. Mercy．．．．．．．．．．．．．．．．．．．．．．．．．．．．．．．．．．．．．．．43
9. Tenderness．．．．．．．．．．．．．．．．．．．．．．．．．．．．．．．．．．．49
10. Peace．．．．．．．．．．．．．．．．．．．．．．．．．．．．．．．．．．．．．．．55
11. Planning．．．．．．．．．．．．．．．．．．．．．．．．．．．．．．．．．．．．．61
12. Encouragement．．．．．．．．．．．．．．．．．．．．．．．．．．．．．．65
13. Brother．．．．．．．．．．．．．．．．．．．．．．．．．．．．．．．．．．．．．．71
14. Servant．．．．．．．．．．．．．．．．．．．．．．．．．．．．．．．．．．．．．．75
15. Self-Mastery．．．．．．．．．．．．．．．．．．．．．．．．．．．．．．．．．．81
16. Trust．．87
17. Forgiveness．．．．．．．．．．．．．．．．．．．．．．．．．．．．．．．．．．．93
18. Gratitude．．．．．．．．．．．．．．．．．．．．．．．．．．．．．．．．．．．．．99
19. Greatness．．．．．．．．．．．．．．．．．．．．．．．．．．．．．．．．．．．．105

Duc in altum

Into the deep
Luke 5:4

Dedication

In 2020 I was asked to contribute a chapter to Robert Falzon's book *Raising Fathers. Fathering From the Frontline. 12 Men's Stories* (Connor Court Publishing, 2020), in which I wrote of three father-figures from my life. Each of those figures personifies a particular characteristic that I have tried to emulate in my own life as a man and as a father: my dad, who has provided a permanent loving and affirming presence since I was a boy; Pope John Paul II, whose heroic witness and commitment to the truth has inspired and guided me since I was a youth; and Michael D. O'Brien, whose writing and words of personal encouragement have nourished me as a husband, father and servant of the Gospel since I was a young man.

At the time of writing, I wanted to include as one of my father-figures in that chapter, Cardinal George Pell, who at that moment was still inside his 404-day incarceration in jail, his public reputation in tatters, prior to the extraordinary 7-0 exoneration by the High Court, which cleared him. I had visited him in the Melbourne Detention Centre on 3 June 2019, totally confident of the falseness of the accusations levelled against him, and found him to be, as was typical, in good humour, cheeky, and invariably interested in the people and projects of my life. He was entirely devoid of self-pity and, as always, I experienced him as father, priest, and close friend.

I first met Bishop George Pell in April or May of 1990 after attending the "Walk for Mary" event, linking the Anglican and Catholic Cathedrals of Melbourne, having sought him out with my brother at a time when two of my brothers - Paul and Dave - and I were seeking advice and support for our fledgling parish ministry. I was twenty at the time and playing professional football for Hawthorn in the Australian Football League, I'd just concluded a three-year Degree in Humanities, and was taking a gap year before taking up studies in education, which enabled the prayer meeting and associated ministry activities to extend into three nights per week. The supportiveness of the bishop, and the friendship which grew, led him to cheer alongside Annie at the MCG when my Hawks won the 1991 Premiership, football being one of many common points of interest, and he subsequently celebrated our wedding twelve months later, came for dinner many times over the years, and opened up many important horizons for me.

It was he who invited me to take up the role of Director of Catholic Youth Ministry in 1996, while I was still playing football, and there I learnt many things about leadership, evangelisation, and fatherhood from him, via his example and his advice. It was under his leadership that I undertook to organise the Jubilee Year 2000 World Youth Day pilgrimage of 400 pilgrims from the Archdiocese of Melbourne to Rome, which was the first of seven World Youth Days to which I have led groups, the most recent being in July/August of this year 2023 to Lisbon, the most notable being the Sydney 2008 World Youth Day, in the role of Director of Evangelisation and Catechesis for the WYD08 Organising Committee, again under the incredible leadership of the Cardinal.

The Cardinal had invited me to Sydney in 2003, at the end of our three-year stint of living in Rome while leading the Emmanuel School of Mission, in order to take up the role of Convenor of Chaplaincy at the University of Sydney. Annie was by then pregnant with our fifth child, and we wished to return to Australia, and the Cardinal shrewdly spoke of his proposal to Annie before mentioning it to me, having a good grasp of the dynamic between us, she being the "rudder" to my "sails". Both Jerome and Ambrose were subsequently born in Sydney and baptised by the Cardinal at the chapel of the Seminary of the Good Shepherd where we lived in one of the houses at the back. The three years of chaplaincy led into the three years of working for the Sydney World Youth Day, prior to our return to Melbourne in December of 2008. We kept close contact in the following years, and he encouraged me in my education and ministry roles, stayed interested and close to us as a married couple, and maintained a fatherly presence in the lives of each of our children. He established his own relationship with each of them, and periodically we would get news of him meeting or eating with them, or from one or another in Rome, or Sydney, or some such place, always accompanied by stories of a joyful edification, learning, encouragement and, when needed, gentle correction.

He has always been a source of wisdom and truth, having introduced me to various important writers and writings. For example, he encouraged me to read the *Confessions* of Saint Augustine, he gave me a copy of *Father Elijah* by Michael O'Brien (I've subsequently devoured every book he's written), and he and I shared spy novels or other good works of fiction (I'm proud to say he occasionally recommended to me an author which I had been the first to introduce to him, but he had forgotten, such as C.J. Sansom). He would share articles that he'd written, or he wanted me to read, as well as drafts of Synod documents in which he was participating, for my reflection or comment. He has been a great supporter of my call in the Emmanuel Community, having also benefitted personally by attending retreats in Paray-le-Monial, and meeting various priests or other missionaries of Emmanuel during their visits to Melbourne, or his to Rome. From the outset his discernment has been practical and helpful, often blunt - which was good for me as an overly spiritual and unpractical young man - and his down-to-earth advice concrete. As I look back, I think of his advice being not unlike Saint Francis de Sales' - immensely human, and while appreciative of human fragility, always based on the highest good for the person, often challenging, spiritually authentic in an "incarnated" and pragmatic way and, without fail, consistent with the doctrinal and moral teaching of the Church.

On 3 November 2022, I was in Rome travelling with my two youngest sons - Jerome (then 19) and Ambrose (then 16), on a European journey of three weeks that was originally meant to take place in March 2020, but was put on hold due to all the restrictions that came with the onset of Covid. We had lunch with the Cardinal, and, in typical fashion, he was immensely generous with his time, giving us four hours. It is quite unusual that the highlight for two teenage boys of a three week holiday in France and Italy would be a slow lunch with a 79-year-old priest, and yet it was a most wonderful time of good food (the Cardinal had no qualms enjoying good food!), instructive and entertaining conversation, broad-ranging topics, fascination with - and advice about - the particular interests and directions of my sons, and lots of laughter. There was no indication that he would pass from this world less than two months later, so I am immensely grateful to God that we were given that opportunity to spend that time with him in person so close to his departure for the eternal glory of the Communion of Saints.

Thus, I wish to dedicate this book to him, a true father of mine. In doing so, I want to make one further observation, and one that in the many things said or written about him that I have come across since his death seems insufficiently mentioned. Many have commented on Cardinal George Pell, the erudite scholar, the sportsman, the priest, the leader, the visionary, the great manager, the humanist, the astute businessman, the connector, the defender of the faith, the falsely accused, and so much more, but I want to emphasise that he was an incredibly masculine man, with a rare integrated personality. A man of warmth, a good man. A man's man. A giant man!

And so, to this book. During Covid I set out to write this book for my sons - Dominic (now 26, and married to Victoria, with a baby daughter, Naomi), Jerome (now 20, at university), and Ambrose (now 17, in his senior years of school) - to provide advice, fatherly advice, on being a man. I intended to make it available to other men who could benefit from receiving from the likes of Cardinal Pell what I have received.

My sons have given me permission to share this book with you. Granted, as you hold it, you will realise that it is a tiny book. May it help you with your life purpose of becoming, in your own way, a giant man.

29 August 2023
Martyrdom of St John the Baptist

Foreword

When I set out to write *The Tiny Book for Giant Men* I decided to write simply from my heart, what I knew I'd been given by God, and what had been distilled over the experiences of my life. I wanted to write of many things I had spoken of when addressing groups of men, and which I had seen were well received, and which I knew were carried by God's grace to inspire, to heal and to transform.

And so I thought, how do I be true to what I want to write? How do I be faithful to communicating what I've been given? After some consideration, it became very clear to me that if I wrote to my sons then I'd do it in a way that was truly born out of a desire to seek the very best for them. I would not be writing abstractions, but offering practical fatherly advice which I hoped would bear fruit not only in the immediate circumstances of their lives, but in eternity.

I, therefore, bought a journal and determinedly set out to hand-write the whole book within the pages of that journal, thus deliberately choosing to keep it short. I did not map it out or plan. I let it be born from prayer and allowed a key theme to emerge for each chapter. I developed each theme with advice and personal stories, sprinkled with references to Scripture and the testimony of saints, added what I have learnt, and outlined the graces I have received. I literally wrote the book from front to back, then having it typed out, I tidied up its many minor errors of expression and punctuation and made the occasional amendment to content. I kept the essentials of what I believe is my fresh, direct, and personal voice.

You will marvel, as I do, by how wonderful God has been to me, and to others through me. My life is simply a miracle! God has brought about quite extraordinary accomplishments in my life: a beautiful marriage with Annie and six glorious children; a successful professional football career with crowning achievements; rich and fruitful experiences of ministry and education across the globe; and unexpected growth and expansion of capacities for adventure, business, and relationships. All this while being a poor, wounded sinner, totally dependent on mercy and grace.

I, therefore, offer you, dear brother reader, what I wrote to my sons, having received their permission to share it more widely. My prayer is that it helps you, even in a tiny way, to become the man God created you to be.

22 October 2021
Feast of Saint John Paul II
Year of Saint Joseph

Chapter One

Freedom

My dear sons Dom, Jerome, and Ambrose, I undertake to write this little book to you as a guide for your life and especially about how to be a man of God in this turbulent world of ours.

It is true, I really don't know where to begin or how to approach this task, which has been in my heart to do so for some months now. It may appear strange or even negligent that I write this to you and not your sisters, but it seems to me that by addressing manhood as a topic, and by providing what I hope is insightful advice that will assist you in that adventure, it will therefore serve them too. Clearly, although I address this book to you, my beloved sons, I choose to expand the pegs of our tent to other men, and so to offer my fatherhood to them. Thus, this work, whilst first and foremost a gift to you, has an eye on the men of our times and - who knows? - possibly the men of the future, if indeed this work somehow survives. Nevertheless, as I believe men have a crucial and, in some way, primary role in renewing family life, Church and society - and will do this by a Christ-like manner of serving, honouring and sanctifying women, and of chivalrously laying down their lives for women - then clearly this book also has in mind the needs and the good and the ultimate purpose of women.

Allow me to begin, as does the Word of God, with the question of freedom. The Ten Commandments are set out by God for freedom. The first and greatest commandment begins with the words "Listen, Israel... I am the Lord your God who brought you out of the land of slavery in Egypt, you are to have no other gods except me" (Deut 6:4, Ex 20:2-3). God is emphasizing that He works for our freedom, to keep us from slavery in all its forms, and if we listen to His Word, follow His commandments, and do His will, then we will be free. This message is consistent with that given to Adam and Eve in the garden, to eat any tree but not the "tree of knowledge of good and evil" (Gen 2:15). What Pope Saint John Paul II says this means, is that they are not to determine for themselves what is good and evil but to obey God. The devil sowed doubt and mistrust into their hearts, and they disobeyed, and as a result they entered into the experience of sin, woundedness, slavery and death. It was Saint Paul who said, "the wages of sin is death" (Rom 6:23). He also showed how Jesus, even though he was God, chose freely to enter into our wretched state by "taking the form of a slave" (Phil 2:7). The fundamental problem of the human condition is sin, our slavery to sin, the fruit of which is human dis-integration, division, woundedness and death.

Thankfully, my beloved sons, though sin is very real, it does not have the final word. If we live the Commandments, we live in the truth, we live in Gods' light, and we live in the Spirit. Jesus himself came to show us, and to bring us that possibility, which He declared very early in His public ministry. He said, quoting Isaiah, which He knew applied to himself, "the Spirit of the Lord is upon me, for he has anointed me, he has sent me to proclaim good news," and, most notably for us, "liberate captives" (Lk 4:18)! Jesus is all about freedom, which is not surprising, because he is the same God who gave the Ten Commandments on Sinai, and who created the universe, and who breathed life into Adam and Eve. The gospels are full of abundant evidence that Jesus came to exercise God's power to bring authentic freedom, through healings, exorcisms, preaching and teaching: freedom from sickness, freedom from the influence of evil spirits, freedom from ignorance and despair. His death and resurrection bring freedom from sin and death. The establishment of a new and eternal covenant "People of God" – empowered by the Spirit of God - frees the people to witness to the world of these marvels of God. The history of the Church, especially through the lives of the saints, continues to show the light of God shining in an otherwise dark and imprisoned world.

My sons, may you be counted among that number of saints, trusting in God's freeing power to save, throwing yourself upon His mercy whenever you are in need, never doubting His goodness, and allowing Him to live in you, so that you would walk as "children of the light," as Saint John would call you. Let freedom be your constant goal. And thus, that you would be truly free, and not deceived like so many of our time who are given over to every whim and politically convenient view, place yourself in the truth that God reveals, and which is consistent with reason. Jesus said, "you will come to know the truth and the truth will set you free" (Jn 8:32). Truth is essential for freedom. So much slavery has resulted from falsehood, even very well-intentioned people are serving the devil via accepting the many deceptions he offers. When I was twenty years old, I begged the Lord that I would never hold true anything that was false. I asked God to put on my path people, opportunities, materials – books or videos etc. – that corrected me and put me in the truth. That year I met the Emmanuel Community and a young Bishop George Pell, both of which have proved vital in my life in truth. Live the truth in love, speak the truth in love. Pierre Goursat, founder of the Emmanuel Community, prayed everyday a passage from John's Gospel that sums up this call to freedom:

> I am not asking you to remove them from the world, but to protect them from the evil one. They don't belong to the world any more than I belong to the world, consecrate them in the truth. Your word is truth (Jn 17:15-17).

My sons, heaven is our home, not this world. We must live in it though, witness in it, just as Jesus did. God has prepared a place in heaven for us, and that is where our eyes ought to be fixed. The devil seeks to deceive, ensnare, and destroy us. Let's be clear, as Saint Peter said, "the devil is prowling around like a roaring lion looking for someone to devour" (1 Pet 5:8). The weapon of protection is the Word of God, which is our truth – and we can be confident of it from Scripture, Tradition, and the Magisterium. Let your lives, my sons, be consecrated in the truth, and so, let yourselves live in freedom, freedom from sin and evil, and freedom for love, service, and witness.

Chapter Two

Purpose

My beloved sons, as you know, I love to call you "beloved" – just as I was always called that by my dad, and continue to be, even though he is eighty-eight years old, and I am fifty-one! This follows the example of God Himself, for at the baptism of Jesus the words from heaven were heard: "you are my beloved Son" (Mk 1:11). These words are then reiterated to the chosen three, Peter, James, and John, when spoken about Jesus from the Father at the transfiguration on Mount Tabor, "this is my beloved Son, listen to him" (Mk 9:7).

It is my desire that each of you would find and follow your unique purpose and path. "To love is to seek the good of the other for his own sake," according to a definition attributed – I think – to Saint Thomas Aquinas. And so, as my beloved sons, it is not my place to impose my vision of your life onto you, but rather to guide, equip and encourage you to follow God's purpose, whatever that may be. It is He who has gifted you with the qualities you have, your intelligence, personality, strengths, passions, aptitudes, and abilities. While I may be your father and Annie your mother, as co-creators with God we're stewards, not owners, of your growth, direction, and development. We will do all we can, even as you become adults, to support you and to help you grow in virtue and holiness, but it is you who must make your decisions, to follow your dreams, to take risks and to make mistakes, and to discover - in the adventure of life – what it is you are created for, what brings you to life, how you can serve others and make a gift of yourself.

There is a wonderful story in the Gospel of Luke (cf. Lk 2:41-52), which I find, as a father, very instructive on many levels. In it we see Jesus as a young person travelling with his family on pilgrimage to Jerusalem for the great Feast of Passover. He is twelve years old, the beginning of adolescence, and it is the only story we have of his youth, thus representing, I believe, his whole youth. He next appears at the age of thirty, the time when, according to Jewish practice, he was old enough to be a rabbi, the same age psychologists tell us a person's identity is formed. And three days later they find him among the teachers of the Law in the Temple. It is this process of pushing away from his parents to discover his own identity that is validated for teens and adolescents. Each of you needs to become your own person, even if family practices, culture and perceived expectations press in on you. Do this without fear of disappointing us but always seek to be faithful to God, to finding your true purpose in Him.

Alongside of the courage you'll need to muster for the adventure that God is leading you, see also that Jesus returned to Nazareth with Joseph and Mary, and lived under their authority. Honouring and obeying your parents in their legitimate oversight of you, is a way of allowing God's authority to be mediated to you, as is true with all legitimate authority (keeping in mind that authority which requires you to act contrary to God's Law is not legitimate, and you must discern how to reject such falsehood).

Parents, of course, must be careful not to drive their children to resentment, as Saint Paul teaches, so we have to pray for wisdom, prudence, and justice in how we lead you. Even in our imperfection, however, we represent God's "authority", a word which means to "make grow" (Latin. - "*auctoritas*"), which is why Jesus lived under the authority of his parents, and thus "grew in wisdom, age and stature" (Lk 2:52). As parents, therefore, we are called to exercise authority over you, and in the same way allow you greater and greater capacity to take more decisions, to exercise more responsibility, and to have more freedom. The parameters have changed since you were babies, and we have learnt along the way how best to balance what appear to be contradictions, but which are in reality two sides of the same coin - freedom and authority. True authority respects freedom, and true freedom respects authority.

Remember, beloved sons, that even when I get old, I will always be your father, so please respect me in that. And recall also that the fourth commandment is the only one with a promise attached to it: "honour your father and your mother, and you will have a long life in the land of the living" (Ex 20:12). More than feeling this as a burden, though, let it be a reminder of how much we love you, of how much we believe in you, of how much we delight in who you are and what you are becoming. We look on you with joy, with approval, with the excitement of the eyes of the Creator, the Heavenly Father, whose affirmation never stops resounding: "You are my son, the beloved!"

May the life you choose to live each day as both a gift to be received and a task to be accomplished, be a "yes" to that Divine Love.

Chapter Three

Being and Recreation

Tomorrow, my sons, it is Father's Day, and I write this section once again sitting in my large leather Chesterfield chair in the lounge, fire roaring, thousands of books surrounding me. The sun is shining warmly onto my shoulders, and with it the light is streaming into the room, vibrant green gum leaves filling the windows in front of me. It is finally spring in Melbourne, after a long and (Covid-related) oppressive winter. Buds are blooming on trees, flowers are brightly hosting enthusiastic bees, birds are chirping in the breeze, and the garden work that for months has seemed hard is now performed with ease.

Thus far I have spoken (or written) to you of freedom and purpose, of living in that freedom which God intended for his children, and of finding your own way within it, based on all He has and will continue to equip you for it. I want, today, to emphasize the pleasure and joy of life lived in Him, of the value and joy of being, simply being. And how who we are is of foundational value, ahead of what we do, and that our first priority is relational, of abiding in God, and of abiding in one another, and of abiding in the creation. For this reason, I want to encourage you to always give prominent place in your life to recreation, and to holidays, because we are called to play and to enjoy, to delight and to be recreated. And all of this is an extension of our first priority as human beings, that is, to worship God. Recreation and worship go hand-in-hand. Always put God first, make sure you make Sunday a holy day, worshipping, glorifying and praising God our Father, through Holy Communion with Jesus in the Eucharist, and by making an offering of thanksgiving in the Holy Spirit, so that your lives may be holy and fruitful! This is the first!

First, let me focus on the recreational element, the games, the holidays, and fun. This morning, being Saturday, you – Jerome and Ambrose – slept in and then at around 10:30am, after I'd been to the shops for supplies, you ate what I would have to say was a glorious breakfast. This breakfast was particularly amazing – eggs, bacon, hash browns, fresh crusty bread, mushrooms, spinach, and tomatoes, cooked on the barbecue, with fresh orange juice – in honour of your (Jerome) second place at the Lawrence family quiz night two weeks ago. This we did via Zoom, joined by Han, Dom and Victoria, and Alex Leach. I designed the quiz, five rounds of ten questions, a different category for each of the ten questions, and it was a hugely competitive and thoroughly enjoyable night. Dom, you came out the winner, and so received your prize of a $20 Uber voucher, already consumed at a movie night with Victoria last weekend, and Alex Leach has yet to receive his third-placed prize of Guylian chocolates but will do so soon. These moments are what join us together and knit a fabric which strengthens our unity.

It is for this reason that I accepted your invitation to play a game of Spy Alley late this morning. Being a connoisseur of espionage novels as one of my favourite pastimes, I am not surprised that I won both games we played, though I can understand that you both thought I was a "fluke" or a "cheat". Family board games have long been a favourite activity, as you well know, both on holidays at Phillip Island, or on the weekends. Whether it be Monopoly, Balderdash, Articulate, Scrabble, Battleships, Chess, or Euchre, we have enjoyed each other's company for many hours, just playing together and having fun. Physical activities too have been, and I hope to continue to be, part of our family culture, and I pray they be always part of yours – whether it be kicking the footy, going for walks along the beach, swimming, riding bikes (like we've done a lot lately), throwing a Frisbee, or surfing.

One of the greatest pleasures in the life of a dad is to see his children take their first steps, to learn to take off on their own on the bike (having run alongside it again and again) or to see them frolicking confidently in the waves at the beach. I have in mind an image of you Dom, catching a wave on your boogie board, and thrusting forward as it crashes, staying up and ahead of it, your face beaming victoriously as you gradually slow near the sand after a forty or fifty metre flourish. Or of you, Jerome, raising your arms in triumph after bending a football miraculously around an impossible angle through the goals from forty metres out, right on the boundary line. Or you, Ambrose, as master of the kayak, unafraid of falling off or of going out into the deep, at times lying down and closing your eyes, drifting, so perfectly at home on the water. Magnificent!

And then there is the joy of having you make discoveries about creating culture, such as we have all enjoyed so much with the "reveal" of each person's Kris Kringle on Christmas day. There you are encouraged to make a gift for your person, and the poems, paintings, songs, stories, and other creative works produced, are all indications of the priority that holidays afford to leisure and recreation, which is the basis of culture. Dom, I love to see your passion and ear for music develop. Little did we know that when Harold Kuipers gave you that little blue toy guitar as a two-year-old in Rome at ESM for your birthday that you would eventually not only be able to play violin, guitar and keyboard, but that you would write songs, translate songs, and unite people in the making of beautiful music, and do so with such a love of the Lord. Jerome, your beat boxing is such a pleasure to listen to, and your designer's eyes, to know how to make a flyer look so crisp, or the cover of a book so simple and appealing, fills me with wonder. (Yes, red, black, and white do seem the best colours for book covers, you are right!) And Ambrose, your ability to not only devour books, but enjoy a range of styles from as basic as Tintin and Asterix, through to Tolkien, Solzhenitsyn, George Orwell, and C.S. Lewis. And now, your articulation of an argument, your description of an event, or your vivid imagination, simply amaze me. That first line of a story you started to write as a ten-year-old still staggers me, and I do hope one day that a novel is published that begins with it: "Vladimir the monk was no ordinary monk, he was a secret agent."

These examples illustrate, among many others I could have chosen, the importance of time spent in recreation, of creating space for the conception of such ideas and bringing them to fruition. It is a co-creation to develop culture. It is not self-determined production, as if it were simply an exertion of the will. No, we are not purveyors of a Nietzschean worldview. We recognise that life and culture are always a form of incarnation, of God entering the created reality, of uniting our spirit and capabilities to grace. For this reason, the truest fruitfulness of your activities, my dear sons, will always be born out of a life that is steeped in prayer and in worship.

When asked how it was that she achieved so much, Mother Teresa answered, "I pray". It seems that those cultures of Europe where art, architecture, and culture are most attractive, are the ones where a truly Catholic view of worship, rest, recreation are deeply embedded, and here I mean especially Italy, France, Spain, Portugal, Croatia, Poland. Let these places teach you that sanctity is nourished by scenery and is seeded in siestas. The Gospel expression, "seek first the kingdom, and everything else will be given to you" (Mt 6:33), also speaks of the creation of culture in a recreation that abides in God.

Chapter Four

Silence

I love the saying of Saint Irenaeus, which states, "the glory of God is man fully alive." While it is intended to mean the "human person," including all people – both men and women – it is certainly true that men being fully alive gives glory to God, and so too does it serve the world. The world needs men who are fully alive, who are full of God's grace, men who are fully themselves, which is only possible in union with God.

Before I begin any instruction to you, my sons, about actions you should take in order to be true men, about work and tasks and the various masculine attributes that are required for you to master, I wish to remain on the attitude of *being*. And specifically, I want to highlight the importance of silence in your lives, and the place of the spirit of contemplation. You will notice the strong connection between this section and the last, which highlighted how culture is born of leisure and recreation. These are ultimately expressions of co-creation, or conception, and they originate in the creative heart of God – or the creative mind of God – and also the creative being of a man (or woman), according to the capabilities, talents and gifts of that person. It is thus a supernatural fusion of reality. (We will come to the question of work in a later section, but I want you to keep this idea of conception in mind when you consider your own work and see it as a holy cooperation with God according to your talents, passions, and capabilities, and to be placed at His service for the good of society and the world.)

Cultivate silence in your lives. This does not mean, as I'm sure you'll know, that you are not to enjoy exuberance, or activity, or that you are not to engage in noisy activities, or have busy periods, or move about. On the contrary, sing, laugh, move, act, jump, dance, work, run, and do all manner of good things, and do them often. But allow yourself periods of interior and exterior stillness, of silence. Be conscious of putting limitations on radio, phones, computers and whatever else may be invented down the track that has the capacity to fill your minds and distract you, so as to allow yourself to breathe in your soul.

Quite early in the ownership of my current car – the blue Ford Falcon V8 – my CD deck and radio broke, and I decided not to have it fixed. This has meant that whenever I drive my car, whether for short trips to the shop or long drives interstate, or anything in between, I am in silence. I use this time to make phone calls, using speakerphone, it is true, but very often it is a time that I sing praises, pray the Rosary or the Divine Mercy Chaplet, or sit in the quiet. Unless I am driving passengers - such as you boys to school or footy training or to the beach, for example, where even then we do pray together a little, as well as chat – that space in my car, by habit and grace reserved for the Lord, naturally invites my soul into prayer. This lounge room where I am now writing, used for family times and a range of activities, because it is a space also reserved for prayer, invites silence and contemplation.

You boys, I know, have your own places and spaces, your own rhythms, and rhymes, and I trust that you will also let silence and contemplation resound in your own way and at your own time. I only want to highlight how important it is, because in short, silence is where God makes His home in us. As the Psalm says, "be still and know that I am God" (Ps 46:10).

It is not an accident that the world was transformed by the monastic movement initiated by Saint Benedict in the fifth century, at a time of great turbulence and social chaos during the period when the Roman Empire was collapsing, and the void was being filled by destructive forces. Prayer is what transforms the world, beginning with one person, bringing about interior equilibrium, and flowing out into relationships; bringing God's peace, love, and service, shaping the world of work, society and culture; shaping economies, politics, education; shaping cities and nations. Mother Teresa said:

> the fruit of silence is prayer,
> the fruit of prayer is faith,
> the fruit of faith is love,

> the fruit of love is service,
> and the fruit of service is peace.

The cultivation of silence is to be accompanied by life lived in the presence of God, who is mercy and joy. I know for me one of the great graces of my youth was when my dad introduced prayer into our home. This took place when I was about twelve years old, and it was a fruit of dad's pilgrimage to Fatima in 1980, and which also helped him turn his heart to us boys. Mary helps fathers love their sons and daughters, just as I'm sure she helped Joseph to love, cherish and serve Jesus. I have written a bit about this episode in my chapter contribution to the book *Raising Fathers*, co-authored by twelve men, but co-ordinated by Robert Falzon, which was published this week for Father's Day. The key I wish to point to is that, for me, prayer was first planted in my life via Mary through the Rosary. Mary always leads us to Jesus, to the Gospel, and to the faithful following of Him as His disciples. She instructed the servants at the wedding feast, "do whatever he tells you" (Jn 2:5), as she tells each of us. Hold onto your rosary beads all your life, holding Mary's hand, and she will lead you always back to him.

Furthermore, let the Word of God resound in your minds and hearts. As is written on my coffee cup sitting currently beside me: "Your word is a lamp to my feet and a light to my path" (Ps 119: 105). Read and pray with the Scriptures, meditate on them, let them shape who you are. Every day, not only by fully engaging them in the context of the Sacred Liturgy, which is their primary place of proclamation, but in your daily prayer.

I must say that it took about five years of praying the Rosary before I truly made a personal discovery of reading Scripture, even though in many of the booklets or other aids to praying the Rosary did I come upon, and was nourished by, little verses of it. I'd never successfully opened up the Bible and read sections, for whenever I tried to it seemed so foreign and unintelligible. Then one day, as an eighteen-year-old, opening up the big New American Bible my dad gave me in the Marian Year of 1987, I read in the Gospel of John, chapter twenty-one, the miraculous catch of fish story after the Resurrection. The scales fell from my eyes, and I understood! I had now entered into a world of beautiful discovery.

My sons, make time for silence, for stillness. Don't be in a rush. Give your time to God. He will multiply your time. He is the Master of time. You make a priority of being still, of being silent, of letting God's voice whisper into your soul. And then watch, something wonderful will grow; it will be marvellous to see.

Chapter Five

Guardian

One of the primary responsibilities given to Adam, as a man specifically, is that he would be the guardian of the Garden of Eden. Men are created and called to be guardians and protectors in their own unique way, and according to their particular gifts, circumstances, and responsibilities. In essence, however, they are to be shepherds for women, and this may mean for their wives, but also their sisters, daughters, friends. And if they're called to the priesthood of Jesus, they are to be a real presence of Christ – acting *in persona Christi* - for His Body the Church, and even more so if they are bishops. In these latter cases they are called to protect the flock from wolves - from those who peddle deception, corruption, and ugliness of every kind. To be a shepherd is to use one's crook to rescue the stray lamb or the lost sheep, but it is also to strike the attacking wolf with the staff, which is the Cross of Jesus.

My sons, whether you are married or celibate, be a good shepherd, a gentleman, but also a warrior who, like Saint Joseph, is the "Terror of Demons"! Oppose evil in all its forms, and don't be afraid of the sacrifice this might call you to make.

The great failure of Adam in the garden was that he absconded his responsibility as the guardian of it. How else do we understand that the beast was speaking to Eve while Adam stood by? Surely there was some form of threat on Adam's life present in this dialogue, in a way not unlike a sweet-talking Mafioso holding a gun to his head. Unfortunately, Adam allowed the beast to lure Eve into mistrust of God's words and then disobedience, a first sin that has reverberated down through the generations. Significantly, after the fall God called Adam to account, being the one whom God had put in charge of the garden, and we see here that Adam had hidden from God, then blamed Eve, who subsequently blamed the serpent.

What Adam didn't do we see that Jesus, the New Adam, did. He did not run from the threat of his life. Rather, he took his proper place and showed his willingness to lay down his life for his bride, as Saint Paul calls all husbands to do (cf. Eph 5:25). Every man is called to be a shepherd, in one way or another, where he protects his flock, his people or his family. True manliness and leadership require that he holds his nerve in the moment of trial. Gandalf the Grey, in Tolkien's *Lord of the Rings* trilogy, provides a classic example from literature well known in our family, standing between the Balrog, that enormous, tormenting, and fiery beast, and the Fellowship of the Ring. Sacrificing himself in a manner to protect the fleeing party, he confronts the menace with defiant determination yelling "you shall not pass," all the while thrusting his staff into the ground, thus laying down the gauntlet for war. On one level it appears as though he loses, for it seems he is killed, but he has saved his flock. And later, returning as Gandalf the White, his sacrifice having raised him to another level, as it were, he became an image of the Risen Christ.

There are many forces in our world today that are seeking to push men to the peripheries, out of their place, so that evil can attack and devour the flock. Resist these forces and take your place! Many men are wounded by life, by fatherlessness, by the scourges of our time, such as drugs, gambling, porn, by lack of confidence, lack of hope, by fear. It is no accident that when Jesus heals the man with the withered hand – the symbol of his masculinity – he calls the man also to "stand out in the middle" (Mk 3:3). The restoration of a man is also the restoration of the capacity to take his place.

I recall in 2008, when I was Director of Evangelisation and Catechesis for the World Youth Day in Sydney when, against my will, I had thrust upon me a key staff member whose qualities – both strengths and failings – worked to push me to the peripheries. This temptation was due to my own wounds and weaknesses as well, the two not being very suitable partners. I was very angry with those above me for this reason, but I can see also how God, as a loving Father, allows us to be put into testing environments and periods of times, to be pruned and forged in ways that require enormous courage. I don't know how well I dealt with the situation, but I know that it produced a combination of failures and successes, one of them being my ability to simply persevere till the end. That very fact felt like an extraordinary triumph, but not without being sorely tested. On one occasion, then Bishop Anthony Fisher said to me, "don't allow yourself to be pushed out," a comment that stays with me to this day.

A comment by Cardinal James Stafford made to me in the same period during a visit to Rome, was also telling. He said, "many people depend on your faithfulness," a statement I have never forgotten. And it is one that brings me back to the call to be a guardian, which is possible only in the mercy of God. Nevertheless, it is a call to courage, but requires prudence too. Jesus himself was not foolhardy, and although he was to sacrifice himself on the cross, he only did it when the Father determined. There were other times when He slipped from the crowd's murderous hands or kept a low profile away from trouble. He certainly never stayed in Jerusalem during visits, preferring rather to be among close friends in Bethany, outside of the city. Discerning which wars to wage is a key dimension of the vocation of the warrior guardian, but having the vigilance and the courage of a watchman must be a man's permanent state of being. "Stand your ground, for the devil your enemy is prowling like a roaring lion, looking for someone to devour" (1 Pet 5:8).

Chapter Six

Presence

One of the most extraordinary aspects of our religion is the nature of the presence of God. It is true that all religions constitute in some way man's search for God, but it is only Christianity that realises God's search for man. In Christianity the invisible God, the Creator of the Universe, the transcendent all-powerful Being, enters into the creation and becomes a human being, and thus makes himself present to human beings. By doing so it emerges that one of us in the human race is God. God makes himself completely accessible through this man – Jesus – who is both God and man. And by doing so, my beloved sons, he teaches us a crucial dimension of the human experience, which is the nature and significance of personal presence.

No doubt you'll be aware of many of your friends' difficulties in life emanating simply from the lack of the loving presence of their fathers in their lives. Fatherlessness is one of the scourges of our times, it being one of the obvious effects of the sexual revolution which drove a wedge between lovemaking and life-making, which promoted freedom without responsibility, and which has left a few generations of children to grow up in a morally confused, fragmented and demoralised society. Whatever faults I've exhibited as a father over the years, of this I'm confident, that you will have grown up with a father who was really present, both physically and emotionally. This does not mean that I have not been absent due to work commitments or missionary endeavours over the years. I certainly have had those when playing footy for Hawthorn, going interstate, or running missions in other countries while at ESM in Rome, or taking groups of young people to World Youth Days! And your wonderful mother carried the lion's share of practical and immediate responsibility during these times as, in fact, she has done this all your life as a bedrock of love and support. However, I have made it a major priority to spend time with each of you as much as practically possible on a daily basis over the years.

One of my daily discernments is to ask myself "what's important now?" I call this the WIN practice, determining at any given time how I might choose to allocate blocks of time, allowing for my primary duties to be realised. One of the ways I might consider this is to imagine that if I were to die tomorrow, and I was looking back on my deathbed to today, what advice would my "tomorrow me" give to my "today me" about the choice I was facing. For example, there is always more work to do in the evening, and of course, in order to do one's work well it is important to meet deadlines and provide excellent services to clients or colleagues, and so giving proper time, attention and expertise is a crucial element of doing one's work well. On the other hand, however, one must never be a slave to work, which has to be put in its proper place, ordered according to one's vocation and mission. So, when you kids were little especially, and even today, I have always made a priority of putting work aside during that dinner time period so as to be really present to the family for bath time, dinner itself, family prayers, stories, and bedtime. Things pop up unexpectedly, and for teenagers, for example, unplanned conversations might arise at the most inconvenient times, such as at 11 p.m. at night. These are the moments when the answer to the question "what's important now?" may be to put aside going to bed and making time to listen to you or one of your sisters talking about those things weighing on you. To put that off to "a more suitable time" might mean losing the conversation altogether.

One of the most significant events of my youth took place when my dad - who himself was abandoned by his own father as a baby, and whose stepfather was cold and distant – came to an after-school running race I was in to see if I would become the school's fourth 4 x 100 metre relay team member. I lost the race but was so comforted in my disappointment by Dad, that I realised being loved was more important than the achievement. Dad had taken some time from work to be there. His presence was a huge gift of that significant moment.

Another great learning took place for me in the early days of our time at the Emmanuel School of Mission (ESM) in Rome. We were living at the Casa de L'Emmanuel in Rome in the triangle between the Colosseum, Santa Maria Maggiore and the Cathedral Basilica of Saint John Lateran, and our home was very much physically inside the school. Hannah was only six, Georgie four, Dom two, and Phoebe a baby. The wall of the bedroom I shared with mum was literally up against the courtyard where the students (twenty young adults from all around the world) would sit and chat in the evenings, tell jokes or smoke. I was struggling very much in those early days, torn between being at home or with the students. If I was in the classroom, I was able to hear when one of you fell off your bicycle in the courtyard and cried. And, in the evenings, when I was with family, I often could hear the students in conversation. Either way I always felt torn. One day I spoke of this struggle with Father Markus Wittal, the priest of the ESM, and he gave me wonderful advice, which was, at the same time, very simple. He said, "When you're with your family, trust that the Lord is taking care of the students, and when you're with the students trust that the Lord is taking care of your family." Somehow, this advice gave me a great deal of interior freedom and enabled me to be much more present to whomever I was with. It helped me to be really present, in each moment, with the person or people right in front of me, to be fully available and not to worry about what was at that moment outside of my zone.

In this I cannot but see the link to what we call the "Real Presence" of Jesus in the Eucharist. It is not simply a symbolic presence, but a mysterious (or "sacramental" presence) of Jesus, as present as He was while walking on the road to Emmaus on the day of Resurrection, even though they did not recognise him; as present as when he disappeared at the "breaking of the bread," New Testament code for what we call Eucharist. Even when He appears not to be present, He is present. In Eucharistic adoration we sit in the presence of Jesus – God who was a baby at Christmas, God who was (and remains) a man, God who was the sacrificial Lamb, and God who is Bread. When He promised to be with his disciples "always" (Mt 28:20) it was in the Eucharist, in his Word, in the Church. By being totally available in heart, He teaches us to be really present to others, how to love those around us, how to bring His mercy, healing and peace to our brothers and sisters.

Beloved sons, let Him teach you real presence, how to be like Him, Emmanuel, who is God-with-us. Christianity reveals a God who is communion, personal presence being at the essence of the Trinitarian nature - Father, Son, and Holy Spirit - distinct, equal, yet perfectly united. A

Communion of loving Persons, fully giving of self, and receiving of the Other. We are made in the image of God who is Presence.

Chapter Seven

Courage

Beloved sons, I write this section on the evening before your sister Hannah is to marry. It is a fitting moment, the fact of freely giving your life to another, to consider the theme I would like to raise here, that of courage. It seems to me that courage is somehow emblematic of masculinity, the virtue that embodies much of what I've already written above. The guardian of the garden, the protector, the one who stands in the breach – he requires courage.

Courage, of course, like every virtue, requires that it be lived with the other virtues at the same time. Temperance – or self-control - ensures that courage does not spill over into foolhardiness or recklessness. Prudence - or right judgement - helps courage to choose its correct battle. Even Jesus, for example, who would offer himself as a sacrificial lamb, slipped through the hands of the crowd which sought to stone him, and evaded conflict on more than one occasion, choosing to enter discreetly into Jerusalem when tensions ran high. He chose his battles and did not need to prove himself to anyone, saying "human approval means nothing to me" (Jn 5:41), knowing that his Father was always the reference point. And justice demanded that he always sought to give each person what was due to him or her, even where this posed risks to his safety, his reputation, or his comfort. Balancing the demands of truth and mercy, as with the woman caught committing adultery (cf. Jn 8:1-11), is a case in point.

As one of the four cardinal virtues, courage stands beneath the virtues of the heart - magnanimity and humility - which help a person recognise, in the first instance, their call to greatness, and at the same time their path to greatness via the humble service of others. The call to holiness, which is both a gift and a task, has inherent within it an extraordinary dignity even though its significance is lived out in small moments and small acts. Saint Therese of Lisieux exemplifies this apparent paradox through her "little way." Saint Joseph too, silent, hidden and apparently insignificant in the Gospels, is in fact a giant in the eyes of God, and the only person of whom it can be said is "the saviour of the Saviour," for he was called to rescue Jesus from Herod to Egypt.

There are different types of courage, all of which can serve to help the other. There is, for example, physical courage, such as displayed by football players, or soldiers, or women in labour. Then there is moral courage, those who choose to do and say what is right, especially when it costs something. Or again, there is spiritual courage, lived by those who follow the prompting of God's Spirit in the "yes" of their trust that He has a purpose and a plan far greater than one can imagine or conceive for oneself. It is this ultimate "yes" that brings both the thrill of adventure and leads to the "Tree of Life," the cross without which one does not experience the resurrection. "Unless a grain of wheat falls to the ground it remains simply that, but if it does die it produces wheat" (Jn 12:24).

In the year 2000 when I was in Rome to prepare for the World Youth Day pilgrimage group of that year, I was graced to meet Pope John Paul II. And on that same day, the 11th of April, I was asked by Marie Barbieri to come with my family to run the Emmanuel School of Mission in Rome, to which Annie and I said "yes". This huge step, which was both exhilarating and terrifying, put our lives on a trajectory that had enormous impact: relating to where we lived – three years in Rome then six in Sydney; work that I did; and harvested abundant blessings for you and all our children, including many graces associated with the people we met, the community life we lived and the various missions we participated in.

I would like to honour Annie, your mother, in all this, as she was enormously brave in accepting to go to Rome – originally for two years – as it meant leaving her extended family at a time when she was a young mother raising four young children. And although she had a fairly good basis of Italian, it meant moving to a foreign country, and having to deal with the children's schooling and all the difficulties of being in a new and unfamiliar place. Then, after three years in Rome, and after a difficult discernment of whether to go to New York to set up the ESM there (something we were not called to do, but would be done by others later), we moved, not back home to Melbourne, but to Sydney. Once again, we had to establish new ties, settle the children in new schools, find our place in the local Emmanuel Community and help build it up. I had to start my new work and, eventually, Jerome and Ambrose came along. This period, after a rich experience of mission work at the University of Sydney, led to me playing a central role in the World Youth Day of 2008, which was both an extraordinary grace and a crucible. At the same time Annie was home schooling the kids. Our "yes" to all this - our abandonment to Divine Providence – was very difficult on the one hand, but on the other hand very easy, and extremely joyful. Enduring the trials associated with all this took courage from both Annie and me. That we were able to do this together was surely a blessing from God.

One of the most important acts of courage that I propose you exercise regularly and unceasingly throughout your life is to present yourself at the throne of Divine Mercy. Specifically, I mean that you avail yourself of the Sacrament of Confession, Penance or Reconciliation – call it what you want - as quickly and as often as you need it. Do not let a month pass without going to a priest to tell your sins and receive absolution. Have total confidence that the infinite and tender mercy of the heart of our Father will remove your sins as far as the east is from the west, and that He will draw you even more deeply into His embrace, and that through it you'll be better equipped to reach out with compassion to those in your life and in your world to share that same experience of freedom and healing that comes through it. Surely it is no accident that one of the first acts of Jesus after his resurrection was, by breathing on his disciples, to impart the Holy Spirit. With the Spirit Jesus empowered them to forgive sins on his behalf: "Receive the Holy Spirit! Whose sins you forgive, they are forgiven" (Jn 20:23). The act of receiving the gift of the forgiveness of God was entrusted to the Apostles who were tasked with what Saint Paul called the "ministry of reconciliation" (2 Cor 5:18). Our response to that gift is to accept it, to take it up, to go to it and to unwrap it. We do this whenever, having fallen, we go to a priest for Confession.

My sons, have the courage and the humility to make this Divine treasure a normal part of your life. Satan and his allies - both in the angelic and human realm - do everything they can to dissuade us from going. They undermine and attack the priesthood, they communicate deceptions about the value of this sacrament, and they sow seeds of doubt, discouragement and distraction in our minds and hearts. Reject all of this, and run to a priest in your need, make it a high priority, never neglecting what is always a transformative encounter with Jesus Himself, in the Spirit, and always leads us to profound communion with our merciful father. It renews us, it establishes equilibrium, it returns us to joy and peace, it makes our relationships right, it makes our work fruitful; it brings us wisdom and returns us to a life of grace. Go to Confession, have courage to speak your sins, and trust that your sanctification is first and foremost a gift made possible by Jesus' sacrifice, death, resurrection and the outpouring of the Holy Spirit.

Never give in to sin! The just man, we're told, falls seven times a day. How can this be "just" if he keeps falling over, you might ask? He must keep getting up in order to fall once again! He doesn't give up. He doesn't despair. Have courage and persevere, even if your faults and failings weigh heavily on you. Keep your eyes on Jesus! When Peter sank after walking on the water, having taken his eyes off Jesus, he cried out "save me, Lord" (Mt 14:29) and the Lord saved him from destruction. Don't be proud, acknowledge your poverty, and go to Him who is the Saviour, who came not to condemn, but to bring us life to the full.

There is that well-known statement attributed to Saint Irenaeus of Lyon, "the glory of God is man fully alive" which I offer for your reflection in relation to courage. Have the courage to pursue the fulfilment of your talents, your strengths, your passions, and your purpose. Make attempts to uncover your deeper yearnings, and commit your time, energy, and resources to excelling and perfecting your skills. Like in the parable of the "Treasure in the Field" (Mt 13:44-46), once you discover your path set about resolutely to give all to complete your journey. That man sold everything to buy the field in which he buried his discovered treasure. It takes time to learn to master anything, so let your courage be realised in the ongoing perseverance of enduring failures and setbacks. As G.K. Chesterton famously said, "If something is worth doing, it is worth doing badly," meaning we ought not to let fear or imperfection prevent us from trying anything. And let us never be an obstacle to another's efforts or dreams. Rather, may you be known, like my beloved Apostle Barnabas, as a "son of encouragement." Discouragement is the work of the devil and his agents; encouragement is the work of God and the Children of the Light.

Chapter Eight

Mercy

This morning, as I was praying, I came upon the following text from the Prophet Isaiah: "Fathers tell their sons about your faithfulness" (Isa 38:19). It comes as part of the canticle of the King Hezekiah, who has just been healed by the Lord after pleading to Him on what seemed his deathbed. In any case, the words prompt me to do as they say, to be a father telling his sons about God's faithfulness. In many ways this whole book seeks to do that, for in the end, it is not our accomplishments or merits that matter most, but the faithfulness of God. And the ultimate faithfulness of God is expressed in and through his inexhaustible mercy.

This book is not a book of confessions, an offering of chapter and verse of all those dreary and pitiful acts that lead a person from the source of life, and thus bring damage, distortion, and death. Nevertheless, allow me to testify that in one way or another I have broken all the Commandments and fallen short of all the Beatitudes. But in each and every act of turning away, or of turning in on myself, in thought, word, deed or omission, I have never been abandoned by my loving Father and God, who forever waits on me, opens His heart to me, and reaches out to me. The merciful, kind, and gentle heart of Jesus, so tender and compassionate to me in my weakness and vulnerability, makes his beautiful and magnificent presence felt, always speaking words of hope, of the future, of affirmation.

There have been many times where I have been locked in the dark prison of my sin where a glimmer of light flickers through its bars, and realising my stupidity, I look to Him and let His rays penetrate my heart and mind, and immediately - in the flash of an instant! – my prison is filled with light, the doors fling open, the chains crash off my wrists and ankles, and He is there, reaching to me with his Hand – its glorious wound blazing – and He leads me away from my isolation back into the Communion of saints. Their colour, vibrancy, joy, the din of life, of love, of laughter, of light-heartedness, all flood me with the peace – the glorious peace! – of praise for Him who is mighty, victorious, the conqueror.

So many times, this has happened – oh, why do I forget it? – but I know, with absolute certainty, that His faithfulness is like a rock, unshakable, unmovable. He will not fail me, and he will not let me fail. All glory to Him!

So, my sons, never despair, never be disheartened, never be discouraged. Simply turn to Him, and He will run to you. He is your servant who will wash your feet – your whole body too - at the hint of a word from you, the smallest movement of desire for Him, for life, for restoration. Even when you have no strength to plead, like the man beaten by robbers on the road to Jericho, left dying by the side of the road, He will come to you as the Good Samaritan, and lift you up on His donkey – one of those who is available to him (may we too be like that donkey when needed!), and He will bring you to his inn, his hospital, to be tended to, healed, restored. He will pay the debt, as He has already done so, and He will bring you back to life. Trust in Him, He is faithful. Let Him pour His oil on you. Open yourself to His Spirit.

His faithfulness comes in many forms. Once, when we were living in Rome, we had been asked to stay a third year at the Emanuel School of Mission, our original agreement being for two. I felt called, Annie did not, and it caused some tensions between us, ruining a few dinners in Rome at what were usually very lovely date-night occasions in pizzerias as Le Monte Carlo or in Piazza Navona. While away at World Youth Day Toronto 2002, and feeling increasingly frustrated, Annie was praying to the Lord for guidance. She opened her Bible, asking, "Lord, should we stay a third year?" and the page opened to this text:

> This will be the sign for you:
> This year will be eaten the self-sown grain,
> next year what sprouts in the fallow,
> but *in the third year sow and reap,* (emphasis mine)
> plant vineyards and eat their fruit. (Isa 37:30).

When she tells the story, she says she immediately closed the bible, as the answer - which she did not want - was so clear and direct. Over time, however, she found her heart changing towards the idea of staying a third year and, by the time I returned from Toronto, reluctantly ready to give in to returning to Australia, Annie felt joyful and excited to do that third year in Rome. Obedient to the call of the Lord, then, and united now in our obedience, we returned to Rome for the ESM students of 2002/3, a year that would highlight in new ways God's extraordinary faithfulness, and which would fulfil that Isaiah 37 text more precisely than we could have imagined.

In October of 2002, with a new cohort of students from around the world (from Poland, France, Australia, the USA, Canada, China, the Netherlands and Caribbean, Brazil and so on), after the introductory retreat of a week in Assisi, each person was prayed over by the others in an act of spiritual solidarity and seeking graces for the year. Having made the decision to return that extra year, it did not take long for the Emmanuel Community to make new requests of us, these based on the experience of a fruitful Toronto World Youth Day (WYD) pilgrimage, and a very blessed international youth forum which preceded the WYD, that took place in English in Pennsylvania. For both of these I had a significant leadership role.

The Emmanuel Community asked three things: Firstly, would I be responsible for running another American youth forum in English in the summer that was to follow, in July 2003? Secondly, would I be part of a team to discern whether the Emmanuel Community would set up a new school of mission in New York? Thirdly, in the event that such a school would begin, would Annie and I move to New York to run it, bringing our family of four young children with us? Having seen how God changed Annie's mind to return to Rome for a third year I was confident such a thing could happen again, because I liked the idea, but Annie was not so keen. This time, however, things would turn out differently, but in the most unexpected manner.

When the students and members of the ESM team were praying over me, unbeknownst to any of them, I was hoping for and asking that God would show the way to Annie about our discernment in relation to these three questions. Exercising various charisms, they were speaking out scripture texts and words of encouragement and words of knowledge, all of them good, but none of them speaking directly to my hopes. Disappointed, and hoping for more, I prayed under my breath, "But, Lord, what about Annie?" After a while it concluded and I felt unsatisfied in what had usually been, on an annual basis, a very rich source of light and strength for the year to follow.

As the students were dispersing from the chapel, and the chapel became nearly still, one student, waiting till I was ready, came up and spoke to me. It was Jerry, a 35-year-old Mexican American from Los Angeles, California, and he said, "Steve, as you know I have really been struggling being here at ESM this first couple of weeks, especially coming from a traditional Catholic background, and finding all this charismatic stuff really hard to stomach." I told him I knew this was the case, as we had already been speaking about it, and I had encouraged him to give it a go. He went on, "Well, I just needed to talk to you - and I'm not sure how to say this - but when we were praying over you I distinctly heard a voice," to which I said, "go on." He said, "And the voice said - you are going to think I'm crazy! – but the voice said, 'Annie is with child.'"

Two things struck me immediately about this. First, I was aware that I had been praying under my breath to God, asking, "What about Annie?" and this, in its verbal structure, was a direct response, "Annie is with child." And second, it was a very biblical expression. It wasn't, "You will be a father" but "Annie is with child."

Now, our youngest child, Phoebe, was by that time three years old, and although we were open to life (and always remained so), we had no plans at that stage to have any new children. We certainly had no knowledge of any pregnancy. So, I said to Jerry, "Let's keep this to ourselves for the moment and see what happens." I told Annie about it, and we laughed together, but shortly afterwards she claimed to have a cramp in her calf muscle, and she said she hadn't had a cramp in her calf muscle since she was last pregnant. So, she went to get a pregnancy test and - lo and behold – she was indeed "with child," as the Lord revealed through Jerry.

We told Jerry the news, asking him to keep it confidential for the time being, and he found it such an encouragement to discover that God does actually speak directly in prophetic words such as in this charismatic gift of a "word of knowledge," but also that He has worked one directly through him which had been confirmed in such a concrete way. Needless to say, this encouragement helped him to decide to stay for the year. Not only that but, once we announced the news a little later to the ESM students and team, Jerry went about saying – "It's a boy, he is going to have blonde hair and blue eyes," and calling him "baby Jerry." (Amazing to think that you - Jerome – are that boy! You are the fulfilment of that prophecy – with blonde hair and blue eyes, to boot!)

Once Annie and I worked out when the baby was due to be born it looked like it was due on the very weekend in July 2003 that the youth festival in the USA was earmarked to take place. I realised that I could not be in America while Annie was having a baby in Rome! So, that answered the first question put to us from the community, of those three questions all relating to mission in the USA. Very quickly we realised, as the dominoes began to fall, that God was not calling us to go to America, but in fact to return to Australia. The answer had come, not just in the prophecy from Jerry, but in the concrete reality of the conception of Jerome, and of its very timing. God's Mercy is amazing!

In order to arrive in Australia prior to Jerome's birth, we had to leave the ESM earlier than the end of the students' year, but everyone was gracious about it. Not only did we have the benefit of the gift of Jerome, but we also had another beautiful baby boy, three years later in 2006, our number six, Ambrose John. It was amazing timing to return home to Australia when we did, because opportunities to go to Sydney - and not back to Melbourne - opened up, with a mission of evangelizing at Sydney University paving the way for my role as Director of Evangelisation and Catechesis for the World Youth Day 2008, a huge one that began in November 2005. It was only in December 2008 that we returned to Melbourne to live – now with six beautiful children aged between fifteen and two years – having departed for Rome in September 2000.

Chapter Nine
Tenderness

I have already written of tender fatherly presence elsewhere, that a man must turn his heart towards his children, and that each must have certainty that he or she is beloved, precious, and the delight of his eyes. Many of the world's evils would be avoided if this were given high priority in the lives of men.

I was always struck by how images of Saint Joseph often portrayed him holding Jesus in his arms. When I was growing up in Australia it did not seem a regular practice of many fathers to do that - mothers yes, but fathers no. And in general, there seems a certain distance between fathers and children in Anglo-Celtic cultures. I know my dad's father left him when he was a baby, and dad experienced his stepfather, typical of the Victorian era "stiff upper lip," as cold, severe, and distant. Miraculously, I always felt great warmth from my dad, received lots of affection, and often was held by him in his arms. I recall when I was little, climbing onto him as he sat in his big chair, nestling myself into the crevasse created by the position of his folded legs, and then feeling his big warm hands on my back or shoulders. Everything about the experience communicated approval, welcome, and acceptance. This was a fundamental "yes" to my existence, no hint of rejection, and I'm sure it has provided a psychological basis for my ability to accept and believe in God as a loving Father, which the Gospels so clearly portray. I am a son of my father, and a child of God. I am loved. All is well with the world.

Tenderness ought also to be a husbandly characteristic, whether as a priest pastor for his people, the flock, or his beloved bride and spouse. As Jesus is the Bridegroom who loves each of us with a tender and gentle love, so too husbands are to be true gentlemen for their wives, cherishing, honouring, and respecting them. This does not mean a husband is not to be strong, decisive or challenging of his wife. On the contrary, the same passage of Saint Paul to the Ephesians calls husbands to love their wives and to make them holy. The demands of assisting one another to become holy have a multitude of practical considerations; to be discerned wisely and acted upon for the good of the other, but in no way do they preclude helping the other to grow in virtue. There are necessarily tensions that may accompany a husband to help his wife to grow in holiness and virtue. And vice versa! To do so in unity and in peace, ideally in a spirit of prayer and communion, is always to be the goal. Annie and I sometimes try to hold hands when we have a disagreement that we are trying to sort out, and this reminds us that the greater goal is our unity, even if this means carefully speaking the truth in love, and listening to each other in love, to find that unity. It often means asking for forgiveness and quickly forgiving. Even in disagreement, though, we are called to be tender and loving, conscious of the incredible dignity and gift of the woman who is our life partner, best friend, and lover.

Having the opportunity to speak in public quite often, and not infrequently alongside Annie, it is one of my great joys to speak well of her in public. I love to extol her virtues and to express my delight in her, my confidence in her capabilities, and my passion for her. I am not afraid, at the appropriate moment, to let people be aware that we enjoy great intimacy. Even at times at home I may be showing her some affection when one of the children comments on it, to which I might respond with: "where do you think you children came from?" causing some discomfort among them. In such a sexually saturated culture as ours, which mostly lauds immoral sexual behaviour, it doesn't hurt them to be occasionally reminded of the beauty, intimacy, and life-giving nature of sexual love within a happy marriage. They might slightly protest, or feign embarrassment, but deep down it helps to embed a profound security. "The Lord is my rock" (Ps 18:2) – it is His love, based on His created purpose, and lived according to His statutes and decrees, which brings fruitfulness, joy, peace and life in abundance.

At the heart of tenderness for our wives is a profound respect for her and her freedom, including whilst we engage in intimate lovemaking. As Jesus the Bridegroom teaches us, when he says, "Behold, I stand at the door knocking" (Rev 3:20), even He who is God does not impose Himself on us, or force himself in any way against our will, or coerce or manipulate. It is always an invitation, always a request: "If anyone hears my voice and opens the door, I will come in and eat with that person, and they with me" (Rev 3:20). Jesus requires from us a free response which calls us to open the door and allow him inside to share communion. So too, husbands are to knock on the door - making it known that they wish to make love - in ways that are both respectful and inviting for their wives. There are mutual obligations, it is true, and no doubt wives are called to "give way" to their husbands "as to the Lord" (Eph 5:22), but this never rescinds the principle of respect and freedom. Many husbands suffer the rejection of their wives and, in this, is a participation in the suffering of Christ whose passion was brought about through rejection by his people, an infidelity addressed in the book of Hosea.

Nevertheless, husbands are called to learn how and when to "knock" on "the door," not only at the moment, but in the days and hours preceding. One such factor to be considered is when she's having her menstrual period, which certainly is a time that she is usually less than feeling well, not to mention having to deal with the bleeding. Emotionally, this can also be a time of flatness or moodiness. In this time, you, her husband, are called to care for her as best you can, and call to mind that her cycle is a God-given process that, monthly (more or less), prepares her for the possible conception of a new human being. It is a rich and vital dimension of the Gospel of Life never to belittle anything of this reality, but rather to hold all of it in high esteem, and to support and honour your wife - both practically and emotionally - in any way you can. Having an active awareness of your wife's cycle, with all prudence, and allowing for her discretion, is an important element of the partnership you equally hold in seeking to be upholding both the unitive dimension of lovemaking and its procreative dimension, that is, being open to life as co-creators with God the Creator. Both dimensions need to be kept in mind when expressing this tenderness.

Just as women's cycles follow a rhythm which have a number of stages, so too is it appropriate for men to be aware that preparation for lovemaking is generally necessary. For men, it is true; God has created us in such a way that it is possible for us to be ready to make love quite instantaneously. This is generally, it seems, not the case for women. They often need time emotionally and physically to get ready. I still recall the example given to Annie and me during an Engaged Encounter retreat, prior to being married, by an older couple where the wife spoke of "turning on the iron." It needs time to warm up, but it will get hot, just be patient. For many years Annie and I have used this code language: "how would it be if you turned on the iron?" might be a question I could put to her in the afternoon, hoping to make love that night. Or she might tell me after dinner, "I've got the iron on!" In these cases, our communication is quite open and clear, in advance.

This doesn't mean, of course, that things might not develop spontaneously and without preparation, which can be lovely. However, if she is tired from working hard during the day (either in the home or beyond) or from taking care of children, then it may be that the best way to love her is to simply let her go to sleep. Additionally, it may also be a moment of disappointment if you expect to make love without flagging it earlier, and then it becomes clear that she has not readied herself. In this latter case, your tenderness may need to take the form of understanding her tiredness or her need to rest and, as such, is one example of how a husband's love can be like Christ, who gave Himself for His Bride - the Church - but whose desires for her are not always reciprocated in the manner hoped.

Which returns me to the fact that men and women are quite different, and that difference makes demands on men that have to consider the best ways that their wives respond. I know that Annie's love languages include service. That is, she feels loved and cherished when I serve her, when I do things that she likes done, such as housework or jobs in the garden. Because I know she likes it when I do those things, I am encouraged to make an effort to try – other commitments permitting – to mow the lawn, or sweep the kitchen, or do odd jobs which are needed. I must confess I'm not brilliant at any of these things, but I do make an effort to do them, and I know that she is emotionally more receptive to me when I do these things. If we have a date planned on a Saturday night, such as going out for dinner, which is a time for being together and sharing - thus a good time of unity and hence leading more naturally to the marriage act of love-making – then it helps me to direct my love towards her by serving her in these ways. I also try to make sure, if possible, to let her have a rest in the afternoon, both things helping to dispose her towards being receptive. Generally, if she feels loved, cherished, and thoughtfully served, then she is open, receptive and close. But if she feels distant from me, not treated well, then that makes it more difficult for her. This whole reality calls husbands to be present, attentive, and deliberate in their love for their wives. There are demands, too, on wives, to love their husbands, but I will not speak of those here.

Regular time together is crucial to keep the life of genuine tenderness, and husbands should take initiative – as well as respond to their wives' initiative – to take moments without discretion or interference. The morning coffee Annie and I have cultivated our whole married life, has become a foundation for so much else. Regular date nights, couple time, and our annual night or two away at a hotel to celebrate our wedding anniversary, all play a crucial role in the ongoing task of building, nurturing or rediscovering intimacy and tenderness.

Chapter Ten

Peace

Ever since I started praying in earnest as a twelve-year-old boy, one of my favourite prayers has been that one attributed to Saint Francis of Assisi, which begins "Lord, make me an instrument of your peace." It was the year of my Confirmation and, in the process of writing an assignment at school on the saint whose name we would adopt, I was captivated by the "Poverello," – by his simplicity, his freedom, his radicality and his passion for everything: his passion for God, for the leper, for his brothers, for the animals, for the Cross of Jesus. Little did I know at that time that I would have the extraordinary grace of visiting Assisi about ten times, beginning with my first trip to Europe in 1990, which I made as a twenty-year-old single man. This was followed by visits there during pilgrimages with young people, retreats with the students of ESM, silent solo retreats of two or three days while we lived in Rome, various visits with children and Annie, and any other opportunity which presented itself while I was making a visit to Rome – World Youth Day business, University conferences or canonizations. It was my dad who introduced me to Saint Francis, he being a Third Order Franciscan and an enthusiast, and who gave me a small wooden plate with the prayer on it. There was also a copy in the red folder – the one we referred to when praying the Rosary as teenagers – which I used to read and pray often. In fact, even to this very day I pray the "Peace Prayer of Saint Francis" at the end of my daily Rosary, and along with it the other prayer of Saint Francis:

> All highest glorious God,
> cast your light into the darkness of my heart,
> give me right faith, firm hope, perfect charity, and profound humility,
> with wisdom and perception, Lord,
> so that I made do what is truly your holy will. Amen.

What I love about the "Peace Prayer" is how simple and practical it is, and how it asks to bring the redemptive grace of Jesus into every situation by recognising the call-to-action as co-operator with that grace:

> Where there is hatred, let me sow love,
> where there is injury, let me sow pardon,
> where there is doubt, let me sow faith,
> where there is despair, let me sow hope,
> where there is darkness, let me sow light,
> where there is sadness, let me sow joy,
> (and I've added):
> where there is fracture, let me sow healing.

The key point here, my beloved sons, is that peace - like holiness itself - is both a gift and a task. True peace is not simply the absence of conflict, but it is the reign of God's Kingdom in this world. We are called to pray for peace and also to make peace.

At Christmas Jesus comes as the "Prince of Peace." As a newborn Babe He is – literally – disarming, totally unthreatening, vulnerable. And thus, we can lay down our arms – and with them, our masks – and allow Him who is "Wonderful Counsellor" to teach us how to bring peace.

I was very touched recently when Georgie took you – Jerome and Ambrose – to Reconciliation at our local parish of Saint Benedict's, where you confessed your sins and received absolution at the sacred hands of Father Dave Tremble MGL. You both came back so joyful, so peaceful, and so full of praise for Father Dave. You both said it was the best confession of your lives. Of course, it is truly Jesus whom we meet in that Sacrament, but the priest is also a blessing. And, as I've often reflected over the years, Father Dave is so gentle, so kind, so much a healed healer, so sensitive and attentive, that he is completely approachable. There is nothing threatening or overbearing or judgemental about him, and so it is very much easier to go to him with those burdens, faults and sins about which we can feel so ashamed or distressed. He is very much like a baby in that sense, like Jesus in the manger, like a Prince of Peace. It is this reality that has so struck a chord in the current world of Executive Leadership through its articulation by Brene Brown of what she calls the "power of vulnerability." The more "impressive" or "accomplished" we are, the more people can at times feel insecure in our presence. So, my sons, be men who are good to the great and the small and make yourselves approachable by your gentleness and vulnerability. And, when you approach others, do so with a smile, with kind eyes, always communicating in all your physical gestures and expressions, that you are seeking peace not war.

This is not to say that you should seek to avoid conflict at all costs, or that you should not be a fighter, or that peace comes easily. On the contrary, to be a faithful disciple of Jesus, to be a man of integrity, one must be willing to be "a sign of contradiction" (cf. Lk 2:34). One must be able to stand with Jesus – who is the Way, the Truth, and the Life – and say, "I have not come to bring peace, but a sword" (Mt 10:34). What He means is that we can never make peace with evil, we cannot compromise our very selves with what is false, we must be prepared to follow the course that God marks out for us, even when that puts us in opposition to others and makes life uncomfortable. To be a man of peace does not equate to tolerance of all kinds of wrong. No, a true man of peace is just, and therefore does not stand idly by in the face of injustice.

It is striking that the person who is praised highly by Jesus above all those in Israel is the Roman Centurion whose clear sense of authority is figured as faith (cf. Lk 7:9). This man is a soldier of the occupying force, a man who built the synagogue in Capernaum and who respected, and clearly defended, the people's right to worship and believe according to their consciences. The true man of peace governs with justice, protects the rights of the people whom he serves, and brings order and stability such that the people can freely live their lives, grow and flourish. This is as true for family life as it is for society, and so the true man of peace has to be a person who is a clear communicator, who listens and who seeks order and consensus, who recognises the uniqueness of each person and their value, who finds a good balance between authority and freedom, and who calmly and freely allows people to live their lives well. And the man of peace has to be willing to go to war against the enemies of peace, but he must recognise that the weapons he uses are to be from God and not from himself. As Saint Paul says, we are to put on the armour of God and to use his weapons (cf. Eph 6:10-18).

In this sense it is striking to consider how Saint Francis, who as a youth went to war for Assisi against neighbouring Perugia (but fell sick on the way), had a vision of shields with crosses on them, and how his literal interpretation was that God wanted him to go to war. Only later did he understand that he was being called to raise up an "army" of Franciscans, poor beggars whose lives were to be devoted to the Gospel of Jesus. Saint Maximilian Kolbe, in a not dissimilar vein, as a young man was captivated by stories of military strategy and saw this as a possible vocational pathway for him until he recognised that the only "army" he was being called to lead was the Militia of Mary Immaculate. Both men of peace recognised a call to war for the sake of peace.

The weapons for peace in the midst of a violent world vary. Sometimes we simply are called to walk away from trouble, to stay clear of a drunk in a bad temper, to remove ourselves from a toxic environment, to end a relationship with a manipulative friend, to retreat into safe havens. God did, after all, send an angel in the middle of the night to wake Joseph and instruct him to take the Child and His mother to Egypt because of the threat of Herod who sought to murder Jesus. Being a man of peace means having our eyes and ears open to God's directives for safety, but also to use our reason to make prudent decisions, for we know that Joseph also made his own mind to avoid Judaea when the angel instructed him to return his family to Israel, because Archelaus - Herod's son - was now ruling.

At other times our weapon for peace is the Rosary. Our Lady is appearing to children in our world today using the title "Queen of Peace," and she is promoting the Rosary as a primary means of making peace. In Fatima she promised that in the end her Immaculate Heart would triumph and that there would be a "period of peace" for the world. Building on those messages, in Medjugorje she has intensified her encouragement to pray the Rosary, as well as to make monthly Confession – her "remedy for the West," which is losing its soul as it loses sight of God – while warning the world that it must return to God as it goes through a period of purification. Father Jozo from Citluk, who was falsely imprisoned and tortured by the Communist authorities in the former Yugoslavia, says that to hold the rosary in your hand is to hold Mary's hand. And, as she is the "easy, short, sure, and perfect way to Jesus" – according to Saint Louis de Montfort in his "True Devotion to Mary" – to go to Mary is to go to Jesus. The Rosary is our weapon against falsehood, and evil. There have been many times in my life when I've been in trouble and without a solution, and I picked up my rosary and prayed, and a solution came, miraculously. I recently heard a story of a Nigerian Bishop pleading for a solution to the dangers of the terrorist group Boko Haram, and Jesus appeared to him offering a sword. When the bishop took the sword in his hand it had turned into rosary beads. The Rosary is our weapon for peace.

When I was fifteen, growing up in Brisbane, as my parents were deep in the conflict that would eventually bring about the separation of their marriage, I was in a very dark place. Each day became a drudgery, as the foundation of my security - my parents' love for each other - was falling apart and crumbling to the ground. From when I was twelve, I had regularly been praying the daily Rosary, and so felt close to Mary, but still felt that God was somehow distant, impersonal, beyond the clouds. Certainly, I knew that God existed, and brought all things into existence, but as yet I had not made a personal encounter in a conscious way with Him. So it was a total surprise, as a fifteen-year-old in a dark place, to have a meeting with Jesus.

I didn't hear a voice, or have a vision, but somehow, I knew I was in the presence of Jesus, who spoke so clearly into my heart, saying:

> I know what it is like for the world to fall down, for there to seem to be no future, no hope. I know what it is like to be steeped in darkness, alone, for I felt that when I was on the cross. But I want you to trust that there is a future, there is hope. This darkness is not the end of the story. There is resurrection.

I'm not sure why, but I believed this was real. I was amazed that Jesus knew what was going on in my life and was visiting me. Things did not change immediately, but over time I noticed that I was no longer in that gloom, and something had shifted inside of me. There was a new peace, and a new confidence.

Looking back, I realise that God first introduced me to Mary, his mother, through the Rosary - which is a meditation on the mystery of the Gospels – and Mary had led me to Jesus. I know it was Jesus whom I discovered is the source of my interior peace. That dynamic of Mary leading me to Jesus, and Jesus leading me to Mary, has deepened and grown over the years to the point that I know that my heart has its home inside the Hearts of Jesus and Mary, two unique hearts but united as one.

Chapter Eleven

Planning

I write this chapter halfway through January, therefore in that phase of looking to the year ahead, coming out of the summer holidays, and getting ready for what lies in store. I have in mind several conversations I had with one or other of you and your sisters about your priorities and goals for your life in the period ahead, and it brings to my heart the question of planning in the most fruitful way. How to best maximise our time, energy, and resources in a way that will best fulfil our unique purpose requires, I believe, wisdom and discernment.

I wish to begin with advice I was given by then Archbishop of Melbourne, George Pell, who was my boss when I took up the role of Director of Catholic Youth Ministry in late 1996. He said, "Do what's important." This was in response to my questions that revealed some unsurety on my part, due to my lack of experience. I have never forgotten that very simple advice and tried to apply it to situations I have faced. Further, I have appropriated the WIN formula – W.I.N. – standing for "what's important now." Basically, if you put in place the important things at the right times you will generally live a good life. Of course, establishing criteria for identifying an order of importance should be determined according to your vocation and duty of the time. During exam period study is a high priority, during holidays rest is a high priority, for example. Time in prayer is always a top priority, so too time with your wife and children. Putting work at a high priority is important, as it is a central way you serve your family and the world, but it should not be detrimental to the good of your marriage or family. The key to this is prayer, not only for wisdom and discernment, but because the Lord is master of time, and He can multiply time. As Saint Mother Teresa would say, a busy person must give more time to prayer. Peter and his companions spent the whole night fishing but caught nothing, and at one word from Jesus - to cast on the other side - their nets were filled with fish.

Therefore, my sons, my advice to you about planning does not come from organisational expertise nor from strategic capabilities, though I know there are people gifted in these areas, and God surely works through them. The ancient Joseph, whose planning rescued Egypt in a time of famine, is one excellent example. My experience, though, is different.

When I was a teenager, it was my desire to play cricket for Australia. I was, following the example and guidance of my dad who played Test cricket for South Africa, a very good cricketer. However, a door of opportunity opened up to me in football when, as a sixteen-year-old, the Hawthorn Football Club recruited me to play for them. I was determined to go in one direction, but God took me in another. Similarly, the opportunity to take my family to Rome for the role of Director of the Emmanuel School of Mission was in no way part of my planning. God led me there, so we said "yes." This kind of thing has happened again and again, going quite contrary to the contemporary wisdom which requires people to make five-year plans or ten-year plans. My personal and clearly lived experience is one based on being receptive to God's intentions. Of course, this works with natural abilities, desires, and requires training, development, stages of growth, links and networks, and a range of other practical and human considerations for, as Pope Benedict XVI said at Pentecost in 2006, the Holy Spirit never acts purely spiritually, but always corporeally, always in and through the Body.

The key to any planning, whether in business or family or in a pastoral and missionary context, is to see where the grace is given. If you are given a child to raise - an enormous grace! – then you have to offer him or her daily affection and discipline. If you are in charge of a pastoral ministry, see where the Holy Spirit is giving the grace, and then put a structure to that grace with timelines, resources and energy. Always remember, it was the Word that became flesh! The Spirit is the animating force, not us or our plans. We must wait on the Lord. We must seek God. We must become less, He must become more, otherwise our activities may well end up being a rather useless set of actions. We must seek to give God permission. The key attitude in all of this is surrender to His purpose for us. Our greatest security is in this surrender:

> Here I am Lord, show me what you want for me.
> Give me the eyes to see what you are doing.
> Give me the heart to desire what you want for me.
> Give me the courage to choose it, and the strength to do it.

It is striking to see how, in the Acts of the Apostles, Saint Paul on his missionary journey is seeking guidance along the way, not knowing where he is going. Then at a certain moment he is prevented by the Spirit to go to Asia Minor and has a dream calling him to Macedonia. This opens up the Gospel to Europe and gives us the pathway providing the letters he wrote, which was his calling. There was no detailed plan, except to say "yes" to the call to take the Gospel to the Gentiles, which the Lord had made clear to him.

Saint Francis of Assisi was no planner, yet the "yes" of his life was so fruitful that eight centuries later we marvel at the impact it still has in our world.

Saint Therese of Lisieux was so full of desire that she was confused by so many conflicting "plans," yet found peace in submission to the Word that illuminated the deeper realisation of those desires.

Have confidence, my beloved sons, for God will show you the way, step by step. "Your word, O Lord, is a lamp for my feet" (Ps 119:105). One step at a time.

Chapter Twelve

Encouragement

Now in the first days of February, and with the new year well and truly underway – Dom, you started your career as a teacher yesterday; Jerome and Ambrose, you began classes at school yesterday, and both basketball and football have resumed; and I gave two seminars last week – so it seems fitting to draw attention to the importance of encouragement, and of why and how we live it.

One of my favourite personalities in the New Testament is the Apostle Barnabas, who was known as the "son of encouragement." It is my opinion that he had a far greater influence on the Early Church than appears commonly held. In any case, I feel a much greater affinity with him than I do for the more intense and choleric figure of Saint Paul, even though Paul is both an undeniable giant and a man whom I truly love and admire. But, Barnabas, I want to emulate, to be like him. And one of the main reasons is because of the way he lifts others up, the way he uses his vocation as an encourager to help people grow. Even before Paul's Damascus Road conversion Barnabas was a leading figure in the Church, and, being a Levite, probably helped a great deal in the interpretation of the New Covenant priesthood of Christ in the light of the Old Covenants. Tertullian held that it was Barnabas who was the author of the Letter to the Hebrews, a position considered "not improbable" by Pope Benedict XVI, for reasons such as those stated above. I am personally of the opinion that he did write Hebrews both for reasons of priestly identifications and their subsequent theology of salvation (Paul as a Pharisee, a theologically trained layman, makes far less emphasis on this dimension in his letters), and for the way his writing suits his gentler character, with its emphasis on a fragile personality conscious of the need for regular and varied encouragement.

Indeed, it was Barnabas who helped insert Paul into his ministry, who recognised the latter's calling and gifts and who drew him into action;

it was Barnabas who helped the Apostles and Elders receive and validate Paul; it was Barnabas who provided a platform for Paul to grow, to preach and to be sent into mission, and who would have helped smooth his rough edges; it was Barnabas who acted as intermediary for the vision that he and Paul had been given and developed in Antioch among the Gentile Christians which was ultimately and formally adopted at the Council of Jerusalem; it was Barnabas who led the first missionary journey with Paul and his presence and encouragement prepared Paul to supersede him for what became the second and third missionary journeys; it was Barnabas who recognised that the time to leave Paul had come when they disagreed about the role of John Mark, Paul wanting to leave him out of the team but Barnabas wanting to support and encourage John Mark, so that the latter would not fall away. At this point we see that God's purpose for Barnabas in launching Paul the great Apostle was now accomplished, and at the same moment we see Barnabas supplying all his gifts and attention to supporting and encouraging the man who - being his cousin and also from Cypress – he had possibly brought into the mission in the first place, and who would become attached to Peter in Rome. From Rome he would author the so-called "first" Gospel, that which is clearly Peter's version, but which we know as the Gospel According to Saint Mark and would be the one to establish the Church in Alexandria, Egypt, where he died a Christian martyr.

So, Barnabas, the son of encouragement, the one who sold his property and gave the proceeds to the Apostles to use, helped to raise up the Apostle Paul, restore the Evangelist Mark and help him find the right path, and was a pivotal player in the diplomacy and doctrinal development at the first major Council of the Church. His charism of encouragement, focussed on how best to raise others up - to give courage that they take steps true to their nature and call - is a grace I put to you to emulate for others.

It was the encouragement of Father Landreth that enabled my dad to take up cricket as a 13-year-old orphan at Saint George's College, Rhodesia, in 1945, by believing in him even when he didn't believe in himself. This eventually led dad to cricketing heights, playing sixteen years of first-class cricket as a fast bowler, as well as a mercurial Test season for South Africa capturing twenty-eight wickets, including an "8 for 53" against New Zealand in 1960/1. More importantly, Father Landreth's encouragement was the sole voice that therefore resounded in dad's impressionable young mind and heart, offered in love and received well. The many stories I hear of Father Landreth's advice about good character and virtue, as well as the spiritual life and prayer, swamp any mention dad makes of his biological father (who left him as a baby) or his stepfather (from whom dad felt little warmth, affection or approval).

I, on the other hand, received regular affirmation and encouragement from dad, from study to sport, faith to character. In fact, I often was made to feel that I was superseding dad, and it was something he would delight in. It seems humility is a key characteristic of those who encourage, as they do not feel threatened, needing to compete, or jealous. Rather, they rejoice in lifting people up. As Aquinas says, "to love is to seek the good of the other."

One of the most important periods of my life, where I needed lots of encouragement to persevere through an enormous trial, was during my time as Director of the World Youth Day in Sydney. It was a profoundly difficult time for me over an extended period, brought about by a combination of high-pressure, mistreatment at the hands of others, personal weakness, and a steep learning curve. In this time, I found extraordinary consolation in Benedict XVI's encyclical "Saved By Hope" (Latin title *Spe Salvi*, 2007), which, when I finished reading it, I immediately returned to the first page and read again. So rich and deep is its content (like almost all of his writing – the gift that keeps on giving!), that I found the second reading quite different from the first. I was pleased to have the opportunity to thank him for *Spe Salvi* when I met him at the end of the World Youth Day week of activities on Sunday 20 July 2008, to which he delightfully responded, "ah, you read zat?!"

Also important for me during that time were a handful of select members of a group I'd put together to assist me to design the Evening Vigil event on the Saturday night of WYD08, and whose faith, friendship and belief in me prevented them from participating in the attempt to sideline me and my work within the World Youth Day office. These included Bishop Julian Porteous (now Archbishop of Hobart), Edwin Bakker, Selina Hasham and Therese Nichols, from whom I felt vital support and encouragement. There were a number of others, especially from the Emmanuel Community, but these others were inside, and had a particular perspective which offered solidarity to me. I have documented some of this in my book *Five Smooth Stones. A 40 Day WYD08 Journal* (Modotti Press, 2010).

Being a person whose major love language is words, I find myself very encouraged by things people say (the contrary is true also), and I'm also very touched by Scripture texts that hit their mark. One of these took place during that time, a text message from my little "sister" Therese Nichols, the fruit of her prayer for me, a message from the Letter to the Hebrews, which was a Word from heaven:

> Remember all the sufferings that you had to meet after you received the light, in earlier days;
> sometimes by being yourselves publicly exposed to insults and violence, and sometimes as associates of others who were treated in the same way.
> For you not only shared in the sufferings of those who were in prison, but you happily accepted being stripped of your belongings, knowing that you owned something that was better and lasting.
> Be confident now, then, since the reward is so great. You will need endurance to do God's will and gain what he has promised.
> *"Only a little while now, a very little while, and the one that is coming will have come; he will not delay."*
> *"The righteous man will live by faith, but if he draws back, my soul will take no pleasure in him."*
> You and I are not the sort of people who draw back, and are lost by it; we are the sort who keep faithful until our souls are saved (Hebrews 10: 32-39).

Such extraordinary encouragement I received from this Word, which fed me for months after that. Even though at that stage I had limited access to the Cardinal, he knew I was struggling, and encouraged me to "hang in there."

The real turning point came for me when I went to the Fraternity of Jesus retreat in Paray-le-Monial (27 Dec 2007 - 1 Jan 2008), six months before the World Youth Day 2008 event. By this time, I had been suffering in an intense way for about two years - so many aspects of my experience as Director of Evangelisation and Catechesis offering for me only darkness and discouragement.

On the first full day of the retreat I bumped into Harold Kuipers, a former student of mine at the Emanuel School of Mission from 2000/1. He said, "Steve, you look awful!" - and I began to tell him some of my woes, to which he suggested we have lunch. We spent the whole afternoon talking, me telling him everything. He was so good to me! And, being a psychiatrist, I found not only a beautiful brother in the Lord, and a man of profound pastoral and missionary insight (he and his wife Daniela have been responsible for the Emmanuel Community in the Netherlands), but also a person with professional capabilities to assist me with my deepest doubts. I had been concerned that I was losing my sanity. He said, "Steve, what you were feeling is very normal." These words, and his long listening, gave me tremendous consolation and confidence, and they opened up the whole retreat for me, where the Lord brought new healing, light, joy, and peace. In fact, amidst the brothers and sisters of the Fraternity of Jesus from all the corners of the world (1500 of them, and wonderful talks, times of praise and adoration of the Blessed Sacrament, anointed meetings, being prayed over, confession, and so on), I received a renewed and strengthened heart.

I was able to abandon everything to the Lord, let go of all my struggles, and – like Abraham sacrificing Isaac - I stopped fighting for what I had been entrusted, such as the Vigil which had been ripped from my hands. Later, these came back to me, renewed, but I was already peaceful by the beginning of 2008, calm, detached. I was now living the advice given by Saint Teresa of Avila, "let nothing disturb you" - I was in a new place. In the end, the World Youth Day was incredibly fruitful, and the Lord used my work fruitfully. Despite some horrendous treatment, I made it to the end, on 20 December 2008, when the office officially closed. It was a triumph that I could not imagine was possible twelve months previously.

Chapter Thirteen
Brother

My dear sons, it is a father's desire to see his sons love one another as brothers. And it is the desire of a father to see each son grow up in such a way that he becomes a brother to many, by his kindness, his friendship, his sacrifice and support. By extension, those who become brothers to you become sons to me, as you have seen, so far as this is possible.

We know that Cain killed his brother Abel, and that Joseph's brothers sold him into slavery. And we saw that James and John wanted the place of honour above their brothers, the Apostles. Malice, jealousy, self-importance can all come in the way of brothers being true to each other. Pierre Goursat forgot his deceased brother until a mystical experience at the age of nineteen reminded him that even death does not sever the fraternal bond. Brotherhood, in fact, becomes for us a litmus test to prove our love for God, according to the Evangelist John (one of the two whose mother – the wife of Zebedee – pushed Jesus to give them places of honour, but who was rebuked by the Lord). In his First Letter it states, "if you say you love God, but hate your brother, you are a liar" (1 Jn 4:20). How we love our brothers, therefore, determines the manner and extent to which we express our love for God.

Do your best to relate well to all your brothers, as Saint Paul exhorts: "Bear with one another charitably, in complete selflessness, gentleness and patience. Do all you can to preserve the unity of the peace that binds you together" (Eph 4: 2-3). You will find this easy at times and hard at other times, simple with certain ones and an effort with other ones.

I grew up with three brothers, Paul, Dave and Mike. I was between Dave and Mike and therefore related more easily with them. Because of the crisis in our family throughout my teens, there was not often a lot of cohesion in our family. Family relationships were therefore not able to be cultivated through common family experiences, such as mealtimes, outings or holidays. Family bonding mainly took place through sport.

Dad gathered us together to lead us in prayer, walked us to school, or coached us in cricket. Mum helped us with schoolwork, drove us to sport, and sometimes from school. But the overwhelming sense during my teens was of a fragmented family (this was not the case in my young years in South Africa and the early years of Wollongong, which were very warm and positive). This lack of stability had a very negative impact on Paul who has always had a tendency to struggle and keep things to himself. When he surprised me by arriving on my doorstep, literally, just after Dave and I had moved into an apartment in Melbourne when I was nineteen, I was determined to make him welcome and make it work, despite the awkwardness of the manner in which it happened. The three of us lived together for a period of nearly two years, the two of them moving out just before I got married to Annie, and much good took place in that time. I often found, however, negotiating with Paul difficult, as I feel I make most of the effort in the relationship.

My relationship with Dave is much closer, far deeper, and intimate, filled with fun, faith and true friendship. This is in part due to the proximity, for he lives in Melbourne and only ten minutes by car, though my family did live in Italy and Sydney for a period of nearly nine years. Our closeness is also due to our common life in the Emmanuel Community, and because Dave is a real living aspect of our family with Annie and the kids. Mainly, however, it is because he and I relate well, have common interests, and both help serve each other. Dave has always been very generous to Paul, Mike, and me, and has a very humble way of connecting and supporting each of us in our times of need.

My relationship with Mike is good, but I feel that I was too self-absorbed, after I moved to Melbourne to play football with Hawthorn, to maintain a good contact. This was partly because I was in a period of recovery and healing from the trauma of mum and dad's break-up now that I was away from it. It was also partly because I didn't know how to deal with the effects of the trauma Mike experienced. (In recent years, things have been much better). In both of these cases, I feel that I failed him as a brother, even though I did make many efforts in my own way, although I know he felt abandoned. The other reason, and a perfectly good reason I did not relate as well as I could have, and the main reason, was because quite a short time after leaving Brisbane I got married and had a family with six children, which is my first vocation, and later lived overseas. Overall, however, despite an aching heart, I try to keep in good contact, and will, for example, be visiting Brisbane soon to be with him and to watch the theatre production of "*Yes, Prime Minister*", which he is directing and starring in. The thought of visiting Brisbane brings to mind how difficult it is to see all my family, because of the fractured relationships, and so the efforts to see them always need to be multiplied. It is one of the heavy crosses of my life, but one which I continually try to carry as an offering of love, because I see the healing that has taken place over the years, despite the mess, is rather miraculous, and so I try to work with the grace given.

My sons, as well as your own blood brothers, you will receive brothers-in-law – the husbands of your sisters - and these you are asked to welcome and make your own, as I have done with Annie's brothers and cousins. When you marry someone, you marry her family, too! Open wide your hearts, therefore, to make them your own, following all the principles of the Gospel and sound reasoning.

Finally, and very importantly, find other men with whom you can be "brothers in the Lord," Catholic and/or other Christian, and just good men of character and faith who will help you to be true to yourself, accountable, and with whom you can share your deepest desires and darkest thoughts. "No man is an island," the poet John Donne wrote. Jesus chose Peter, James and John to be his closest companions from among the Twelve, and with them he shared his deep experiences of exaltation (such as the Transfiguration on Mount Tabor) and of desolation (such as the agony in the Garden of Gethsemane). All great men have a few intimates, and a group of close "brothers" beyond them, and then the group ahead of the crowd. It is true for singles, priests, consecrated men and married men. This does not mean the exclusion of women. On the contrary, close friendship with women is also essential! Married men, especially, should find their wives as their closest intimate companion, ideally, but the relationship they can have with "brothers" is unique.

Chapter Fourteen

Servant

My beloved sons, in the parable of the Prodigal Son, otherwise known as the parable of the Merciful Father, it is clearly seen that there are two basic attitudes sitting quietly and subtly in opposition to each other. The first is the attitude of the "slave", articulated by the jealous older brother. His self-righteousness leads him to condemnation of his younger brother and anger at his father, even while the father is doing something quite wonderful as he restores the younger son. The younger son too, for his part, even while returning to his father out of sheer desperation, having squandered his inheritance, seeks in his limited perspective, to be treated "like a hired servant" (Lk 15:19). Just as the older son thought he deserved a place by his efforts, so too the younger son thought he did not deserve a place due to his failure. The father's retort is not about effort, in either case. To the older son he says, "All I have is yours" (Lk 15:31) and refers to the younger son as "this son of mine" (Lk 15:24). As Jesus said elsewhere, "a slave has no permanent place in the family, but a son belongs to it forever" (Jn 8:35). Sonship sits in contrast to slavery. Who we are as sons, each of us, in relation to the father, our sonship is the foundation of everything we do. This truth is affirmed directly to Jesus as he comes up out of the water at his baptism, "you are my Son, the beloved" (Mk 1:11), later confirmed in public, "this is my beloved Son, listen to him" (Mk 9:7).

It is only upon this basis that I wish to highlight the key idea of this chapter, the idea that a true man is a servant, for it is possible that this can be lived as a kind of slavery, if understood incorrectly. And we also know that at a horizontal level Jesus sought friendship over relationships based on action, such as when he said to his disciples, "I no longer call you servants, but friends" (Jn 15:15). This statement does not negate the servant-master dynamic, but rather goes to a depth of intimacy and communion, which is an experience of the heart. The greatest service is love, living the Commandments, putting God first in all things.

It also needs to be stated that Jesus said, "the Son of Man did not come to be served, but to serve" (Mk 10:45). It is this attitude of service which I wish to encourage in each of you, an attitude which seeks to do what is good, to perform your duties well every day, to be responsible with your things, recognising that everything is a gift.

A true servant has a spirit of gratitude conscious that everything comes from God. Service does seem to extend from humility, from an attitude of receptivity, that, because God is the Giver of all gifts and I am called to be like Him, I too will seek the good of the other. Service, an expression of love, seeks the good, is other-centred, it has a sense of the whole, of being a part of the whole, of being responsible for participating in and contributing to society, community, and family. The adversary of God, the enemy of humanity, on the other hand, Satan, says *"non serviam!"* "I will not serve!" Mary, the one who crushes the serpent's head, responds to God's invitation with the words, "I am the servant of the Lord, let what you have said be done to me" (Lk 1:38).

As I write these words, Ambrose is cleaning the kitchen, it being his duty tonight. Annie, sitting across from me in the lounge room, is putting the final touches on her preparation for tomorrow's first session of this, her sixth, Momnipotent program for mums. Jerome is doing his homework in his bedroom. Daily life is filled with basic duties that we are called to perform, and like Saint Therese says, we can do small things with great love. Jesus washed his disciples' feet, a mundane – if unusual – task, and an action which he modelled for his disciples to replicate. At the heart of his priestly self–offering was this *diaconal* action, this ministry of service. Saint Peter Chanel, the first martyr of Oceania, expended himself for the service of his people, and so too do husbands care for their wives, providing love, cherishing with both practical and emotional support to help them in their roles as wives and mothers.

A man's work is a primary way he serves his family and the world, both providing for his family's needs and at the same time making a positive impact on the world by his skill, his effort and the exercise of his gifts. Saint Joseph the Worker is a great model in this regard, showing men about the sanctification of the world through work. He is the patron of workers, not the patron of workaholics, and he is always centred on his family, serving God, raising his Son, contemplating in silence, and is a great intercessor in heaven for men, for families, for practical needs – such as houses, work and finance – as well as spiritual needs.

Annie's dad used to say, "One of the best ways a man can love his children is to serve their mother," a practice he lived out magnificently in their unified marriage. My dad has continued to serve mum, even thirty-five years since their separation, by many times mowing her lawn or fulfilling some such practical fix–it job. When children are little, especially, mums need a break, and this is one way a dad can support and serve her mothering, by providing her with a well-earned break, perhaps physical or emotional, letting her get extra sleep, freeing her to go out and visit friends or get exercise, and to actively look for ways to be truly present to her, to listen, to honour and to cherish her.

When I asked Annie just now what ways she feels I serve her, her response made me laugh. She said that I sometimes choose "yucky" jobs, so she doesn't have to do them, such as putting cream on our dog Bilbo's rear-end cyst, which I'm currently doing, or by doing the bulk of the one hundred and twenty hours of driving lessons required for each of the kids who have driver's licenses (four down, one current, and one to come!) She also mentioned speaking to the children in such a way as to provide guidance, even those in their twenties, exemplified by a phone call today from Dom who is in the midst of a very steep learning curve, having started teaching in the classroom about three months ago. And, my final example, she said she has felt my service by challenging and encouraging her to use her gifts.

Serving comes in many shapes and sizes, and can be exercised at different times, but at its heart is an attitude of being a man for others. This is, in fact, a definition given by Pope Saint John Paul II for the priest – "he is a man for others." It is also true of a husband – "a man for his wife" – and a father – "a man for his children" – and any baptised man, young or old, married, or single - "a man for others." That *being for others,* not for self, has ramifications that require sacrifice and, at times, suffering. Jesus is the ultimate fulfilment of what are called the "Suffering Servant" songs, from the prophet Isaiah (cf. Isa 42, 49, 50, 52), which are applied to his passion and death on Good Friday, for through them he provides the greatest service of all, our salvation.

My sons, despite our weakness and our limitations, in our own ways we too can participate in this act of service of Jesus, by our "yes", by our "speak Lord, your servant is listening" (1 Sam 3:9-11), by our response to his grace in our lives. And as Saint Catherine of Siena has said, "To the servant of God every place is the right place, and every time is the right time." And again, "you are rewarded not according to your work or your time, but according to the measure of your love."

One of the great blessings I received by being a member of the Emmanuel Community is to be asked to do "services" as a normal aspect of community life. All members are given a mission – which can change overtime – as well as services, which can vary from very mundane things, such as to vacuum the floor or wash dishes or make announcements; to something more like a ministry, running the program for the children or teenagers, or being in charge of a Maisonnee (the small sharing group for the year). I was very touched early on when, in Paray, I would see Martine Catta, the co-founder of the community, cleaning tables, or a priest such as Father Terry Quelquejay wearing an apron and a plastic hat while serving food.

A strong aspect of the growth in humility is the humble service of brothers and sisters. It brings to mind the story, well known from the beginning of the community, relating to a young man named Gabriel Priout. Gabriel was very serious and perhaps a little proud, and when he and Pierre Goursat went to the supermarket Pierre jumped into a shopping trolley, with his legs dangling over the edge of the basket, and made Gabriel push him around. It was mortifying for Gabriel, but eventually liberating. He learned not to take himself too seriously, to let go of what people thought of him, and become much more child-like in simplicity. Gabriel became a priest and has spent much of his life as a missionary in Africa. The relationship between interior freedom and service is striking.

A service I've especially come to value over the years is to be rostered onto the children's ministry or teens on a community day. I know how important it is for the parents that their children have a positive and up building experience of those days, and although the children are not members – per se - of the community, I have always wanted to take the opportunity to get to know these kids and the young people, to love them, and to help them to grow in character, in faith and in friendships. It has been very much an evangelising mission, that is, a way of bringing Jesus' love to them. It's what I have wanted for you boys over the years, and in a number of cases – you'll be very aware of them – these people have been very important to you.

Service always takes a person outside of themselves, puts them in a milieu where the needs and demands of others are thrust upon them, and they are thus expanded, developed, and taught humility. The best thing to propose to a self-absorbed person is to find a service, and they will – hopefully – learn to think and act for others.

In short, let it be obvious to everyone that you are a man of service.

Chapter Fifteen
Self-Mastery

On the wall in our lounge room at home is a painting by Michael D. O'Brien of Raphael leading Tobias as they walk by the river. Upon his back Tobias holds a magnificent large blue fish. We know from the Book of Tobit that the properties of this fish bring marital happiness to Tobias, and subsequently great prosperity, and they also bring healing and restoration to Tobit, Tobias' father, whose name the book carries. For these reasons this painting, and the book before it, hold enormous significance to me. Allow me, my sons, to explain, for in this story lies a hidden treasure which I desire you to grasp firmly, not only with your mind, but with your heart and eyes and hands. This treasure relates to the virtue of chastity and the grace of self-mastery.

Tobit is a just man who gives alms to the poor, who is faithful to the precepts of Israel, despite the pressures placed upon him by the Assyrian foreign powers, and who, despite the associated dangers, buries the dead of the victimized Jews in exile. He makes the effort to go to Jerusalem on pilgrimage, thus honouring the Temple of the Lord. Indeed, he is exemplary in the corporal works of mercy.

In his prayer to the God of Israel, he intercedes for his people, and so too does a young woman named Sarah intercede in her need. She had married seven men in succession, and on the wedding night each of these had been killed by the demon of lust, Asmodeus. In reply to the lament of both, for Tobit had become blind due to bird manure landing in his eyes, misfortune having befallen him, God sent the Archangel Raphael to bring healing, restoration, and fortune.

Raphael, appearing as a man, accompanies Tobias to collect money for Tobit from a distant relative, whose daughter was the Sarah mentioned. Surely her self-worth must have been very low, for each time her husband went to consummate the marriage he died. Her life was misery! Along the way they walked by the river, and Tobias sat and put his feet in the water. It was at this moment – this crucial moment – that a huge fish swallowed his foot and threatened to drag Tobias into the abyss. The Aramaic original, according to the Vulgate translation – quite probably the original text, for Tobit hailed from the Upper Galilee region of the tribe of Naftali (cf. Tob 1) - puts as the words of Raphael, "Master the fish!" a most unusual directive. Indeed, in the Aramaic it is a "monstrous fish" which undoubtedly threatened the very life of Tobias. The directive of Raphael is most important, because he does not tell Tobias to throw off the fish, but rather to "master" it.

The Fathers of the Church and many saints have applied a spiritual interpretation to the fish as representing Christ himself as the means by which life is restored, healing given, and providence offered, all of which are certainly appropriate as an interpretation. I wish to delineate in a specific manner, though, that the key enemy in the story is lust, as we see later in the prayer of Tobias and Sarah at their wedding bed, and that this is the monster to be mastered. Instead of throwing off the fish, avoiding the problem (symbolising repression) Raphael – which means, "God heals" – instructs Tobias towards self-mastery, and then, specifically explains that the burning of the heart of the fish will dispel the demon of lust. This is exactly what happens when Tobias, the Christ-figure who faces death in his marriage to Sarah (remember, every man she married was killed by the demon of lust), prays at the wedding bed: "I do not take my sister for any lustful motive; I do it in purity of heart" (Tob 8: 9).

This self-mastery that enables a successfully unified and happy union between Tobias and Sarah, and which brings her happiness out of the misery she had lived due to the lustful objectification directed towards her by her seven previous husbands, is brought about through the offering of the heart of the fish on the fire. This is signifying the power of Christ's heart to save, to liberate, to heal and bring happiness. And it shows also how this grace is a gift but, as we have seen in the Archangel's directive towards Tobias to mastery, it is also a task. Herein lies the mystery of holiness, it is first a gift, and impossible without the gift. At the same time, however, in response to the gift it is a task, it is a battle, it is a war, a war that must be won, but only in and through Christ's heart.

The wisdom literature of the Old Testament tells us that "the just man falls seven times a day" (Prov 24:16). What makes him just is not that he falls, for sin is never a good thing in itself, but that he gets up, again and again. We know that learning from our failures is a path to success. Even King David, who we are told was "a man after God's own heart" (1 Sam 14), was guilty of both adultery and murder, but whose repentance was so whole-hearted that we are left with a masterpiece to use for prayer in our sinfulness. Within the one Psalm, "the Miserere" (Ps 50/51), we see him pleading first for mercy for his sins, and to be washed of his guilt, by appealing to God's tenderness; then to his justice, asking for a "clean heart." In the very act of seeking his sins to be wiped away and to be washed of all his guilt, he acknowledges that "in secret you teach me wisdom," alluding to how God mysteriously works things to the good even through our sins. (Or, as Saint Augustine put it, "oh happy fault, that wrought for us so great a saviour.") He boldly goes on, growing in confidence within the one act of prayer, that the mercy he seeks is being given him, the guilt he wants washed is disappearing, the wisdom he senses he is learning is growing in his very presence, and now - putting his failure behind him - he boldly states, "renew my joy... and I shall teach transgressors your ways, and sinners will return to you." He knows that sin damages us, but he also knows that God restores, "Show your favour graciously to Zion, rebuild the walls of Jerusalem."

Mary Magdalene was weeping at the tomb of Jesus, even while the risen Jesus stood before her! How often we too remain in the misery of our sinfulness and fail to look up at Jesus – who has conquered sin and death by his Resurrection – to receive the new life He yearns to give to us! "Mary," (Jn 20:16) he said to her, and she recognised him then. Let each of us turn our eyes to him, turn away from the misery of our sins, and let him speak his name: Dominic! Jerome! Ambrose! And you, dear reader! The victory over lust is Jesus' victory, it is the victory of hearing our name pronounced from his lips:

> Do not be afraid, for I have redeemed you;
> I have called you by your name, you are mine.
> Should you pass through the sea, I will be with you;
> or through rivers they will not swallow you up.

> Should you walk through fire, you will not be scorched
> and the flames will not burn you.
> For I am the Lord your God,
> the holy One of Israel your saviour...
> because you are precious in my eyes,
> because you are honoured, and I love you.
> (Isa 43:1-4)

After the miraculous catch of fish (Luke 5:1-11) Simon feels his unworthiness of the call of Jesus and says, "Leave me Lord for I am a sinful man," to which Jesus responds, "Do not be afraid! From now on I will make you fishers of men." Paul too confesses his human weakness on a number of occasions, referring to a "thorn in the flesh," which he believed was given to him to keep him humble. Having pleaded with the Lord to take it away, Jesus replied by saying, "my grace is enough for you – my power is at its best in weakness" (2 Cor 12:9). Whether Paul was referring in coded language to a character flaw relating to sexual sin or not, the basic truth is consoling for us men, for whom sexual integrity is difficult and the virtue of chastity an ongoing struggle.

My experience of the last forty years, since puberty, verifies the above. I have been aware of what is right and wrong in this area, but I have also been abundantly conscious of how fragile I am. I know that the woundedness that eventuated from my mum and dad's conflict over a number of years, which took place during what is normally a vital period of psychosexual development, has most probably exacerbated the struggles for me over the years, but I have nonetheless fought very hard to win the battle over lust. And I can certainly attest that it is a battle which cannot be won with sheer effort, no matter how strong a person is. This is where grace is key, which brings us back to Tobias and the fish, and the Archangel Raphael's instructions to burn the heart of the fish as an offering to God. Prayer is fundamental, whether it be the prayer of a married couple, personal prayer, community prayer, or the Eucharistic offering of Jesus' own Body, our sexual drive has at its core our yearning for God, our deep desire for communion – to be known and to know, in the truest sense of these terms. Sex is a deeply and profoundly spiritual reality - lived in and through the body, in our maleness or femaleness (maleness for you guys as men!) – which is realised in this life through marriage or celibacy. In either case we are called to offer our hearts to God.

The heart of the fish, being burnt as an offering, points to, on the one hand, the offering of Jesus on the cross who, as the Bridegroom, "loved the Church and sacrificed himself for her to make her holy" (Eph 5:25-26) as a husband is called to do for his wife. We see this in the Gospel of John, where the heart of Jesus is pierced and both blood and water pour forth (cf. Jn 19:31-37) as the sacramental means of salvation and sanctification. This is what all blood sacrifice and burnt offerings of the Old Testament point towards, and in which they are all fulfilled, as Hebrews expands.

On the other hand, it is also an allusion to the offering of the heart of the Christian, united to the Heart of Jesus. Unless the two hearts meet, the offering of Jesus does not become actualized in that person. We see this in the story of the Apostle Thomas, who absented himself from the community of believers and was thus not present when the Lord Jesus appeared to them on the day of Resurrection, whom we know was refusing to believe. One could say he exemplified the "uncircumcised heart" of those who have not truly encountered the Lord. So often in the Old Testament do we see references to the "uncircumcised heart" and, as its remedy, the promise of a "new heart" and a "new spirit," a "heart of flesh" to replace the "heart of stone." This is what the Covenant of Circumcision is pointing to, surely! The circumcision of a man's penis was God's way towards the circumcision of his heart. Saint John is making this point, I believe, with his specific reference to the eighth day. The Law required circumcision on the eighth day, physical circumcision of the penis, and John tells us that "eight days later the disciples were in the house again and Thomas was with them" (Jn 20:26). Jesus comes to him, even though "the doors were closed" and invites Thomas to touch the holes in his hands and feet, and to put his hand in Jesus' side, which, of course, is a reference to his pierced heart. Thomas, whose unbelieving, hard heart, whose previously uncircumcised heart makes an encounter with the pierced heart of the risen Lord, is thus transformed by its power, completely becoming a new man. This transformative experience not only offers knowledge which goes beyond reason and all that can be attained by scientific method, it also floods his entire being with Divine

Life, so that he is able to recognise that Jesus is for him "my Lord and my God" (Jn 20:28). This transformative experience, and the Pentecostal outpouring of the Holy Spirit which is integral to it (in John's Gospel the outpouring of the Holy Spirit comes from the Cross and Resurrection), pushes Thomas to witness to the ends of the Earth, and to culminate his self–gift as a martyr in India.

The circumcision of the penis leads to the circumcision of the heart, and the sexual drive is thus geared towards its fulfilment in the union of two hearts, a transformative union in Christ's heart.

My interest in, my profound study of the writings of John Paul II, his Theology of the Body, and those who are gifted in simplifying and articulating it, has its driving force in my desire to learn and grow in this area. Since I was eighteen and reading "The Gift of Sexuality" by Father Fox from the Fatima Centre, my reading of Christopher West and Jason Evert, my Master's degree at the John Paul II Institute for Studies of Marriage and Family, and my mission doing "Love and Truth" weekends and evenings alongside Annie, have all had at their core the questions: what does it mean to be a man? How do men and women serve one another in a healthy way? How ought men and women serve one another in a healthy way? How to heal the hearts of men and women in their relationships? How to truly love one another?

Through all of this God has answered a prayer that Dave, my brother, and I prayed so earnestly when I was twenty, "Lord, put us into the truth! Let us have a profound perception of reality, a deep understanding of things as they are, and show us how to live." This, of course, is an ongoing journey of conversion, even as a man in my fifties. The Lord is continuing to ensure I do not get puffed up. All glory to Him!

Chapter Sixteen

Trust

This chapter might otherwise be entitled "Money," as it relates largely to the need for it, a matter of concern preoccupying the minds of men, but I rather would prefer to focus on the trust in God for all things. God, of course, knows we need money, and knows that we, as husbands and fathers, need to provide for our wives and our children, and to share with the needy, if we are to be good men. Nonetheless, as Jesus said, "Seek first the kingdom of God, and everything else will be given to you besides" (Mt 6:33).

My sons, is Jesus offering impractical advice? Is He so focused on spiritual things that He is outside the realities of normal people in daily life? Or rather, is He so confident in the Providence of the Heavenly Father that He knows that if we put first things first – that is, God – then all the rest will fall into place? This is in no way to encourage irresponsibility, or to excuse laziness, or to abscond responsibility. Not at all! Every man must find how to apply his gifts, talents and passions to good use, to the service of others, and to plan, prepare, and take calculated risks, so as to earn a good living. There must also, however, be a sense of awareness that everything comes from God. In short, we need the humility to recognise that even if we are very successful in our endeavours, and should these bring us a fortune, that it is because God has blessed us. Similarly, if we toil for a simple living, that too can be a sign of God's blessing. It is worth noting, though, that the stars in the sky are abundant, and so too the powerful majesty of the oceans. The Holy Family in its exile into Egypt, refugees from the murderous Herod, were provided for initially by the gift of gold from heaven, via the agency of the foreign Magi from the East. The miracles of the loaves and fish always gave more than enough, and that of the water to wine at the wedding feast provided more of the best wine than they knew what to do with. So, my point is, God will take care of your needs, just make sure you put Him first and live according to His ways, which means being simple, being generous, for God will not be outdone in generosity, and living at rights with Him.

My experience is that if you give your life over to God and to His plans, that if you live according to His purpose, then He will bless you abundantly. I was very fortunate to be recruited by Hawthorn and play twelve seasons for them, and I made a priority of putting any extra payments I received into paying off the bank loan on the house. By the time I finished my football career I had completely paid off the house and had no debts. We were also greatly helped by a regular payment that came to us every year from a trust set up by Annie's parents.

Not owing anything on the house gave us the freedom to say "yes" to going to Rome to work at the Emanuel School of Mission for three years, where I earnt very little, but where we had all our needs taken care of, and had the richest experience of faith, community, and culture that one could imagine. It also enabled us to basically make our home in Melbourne available to a few families, for next to no rent, over a nine-year period (three in Rome and six in Sydney). We know this was an enormous blessing to these families, a few of whom came from overseas or interstate to study at the John Paul II Institute for Marriage and the Family. And we know that our generosity to them also became a source of blessing for us.

Similarly, we gave our Toyota Tarago for other families to use, and only asked that they cover the costs of registration and servicing. We held that our possessions, even our house and our car, were ours to share. We are stewards of God's gifts. I'm sure it's one of the reasons God so lavishly gives you kids cars for nothing when you have prayed novenas to Saint Joseph. This is what Jesus means when he says, "the measure with which you measure, will be measured for you." This word is preceded by an instruction about giving: "Give and it will be given to you. A good measure, pressed down, shaken together, and running over, will be poured into your lap" (Lk 6:38).

There are many examples like these which I can share with you. Making your home a place of hospitality is another aspect of this trust, and I mean not only with people whom you like, but also those who are lonely, or in hard times. To invite people to your home, to share a meal, I believe is one of the great acts of love, and, at the same time, of honouring God who provides all things to be shared and enjoyed with others.

I consider that I've been greatly blessed by having good incomes with my work, and even employed by the Church we have always had more than enough money. My World Youth Day and ACU roles in senior leadership were excellently remunerated, and my Mazenod College role was provided for as the equivalent of a Deputy Principal, all thanks to the generosity of: Cardinal Pell, Greg Craven, and Father Michael Twigg OMI, respectively. Good bosses understand that it is important to pay your key staff well, and this helps to get the best out of them, as does treating them well. Cardinal Pell, as Archbishop of Melbourne, offered me a very generous pay as Director of Catholic Youth Ministry, which launched me into my mission of working for the Church, something I did while still playing footy. I never expected to go down that track, but God has always made it possible to live out that mission, as you have seen.

For me the first question has always been to follow my heart and to say "yes" to God's call, even when that has come out of left field, which has, in fact, mostly been the case. I never thought of playing AFL football until I was asked to as a Year 11 student in Brisbane. Founding the Emmanuel Community in Melbourne emerged from our response to a call made in France while on our honeymoon in Paray-le-Monial. Catholic Youth Ministry was an idea of the Cardinal. The call to ESM Rome came from Marie Barbieri – totally unexpected – on the same day as I met Pope John Paul II on the 11th of April 2000, while there to prepare for the Australian pilgrimage to World Youth Day 2000 in Rome. The invitation to Chaplaincy at the University of Sydney again came from the Cardinal (Archbishop Hart seeing no role for me in Melbourne, after our return from Rome), as did my role in World Youth Day 2008. I know that he also encouraged my appointment to ACU, though it became abundantly clear that I was not wanted by those in senior leadership there, a fact that made my experience awful. Even my move into the role at Mazenod was not what I had envisaged, originally, and it took some prompts for me to see God's call there, which brings me to my current role where I now run my own business for Catholic leaders.

Without going into any great detail you need to be aware that this latest move came from a series of acts of discernment (lots of reflection and writing, plus the participation in a Halftime Executive roundtable) that led me to realise I was being called, indeed that I desired, to create a business where I would fully dedicate myself to speak, coach, consult and write for the service of leaders in ministry and education. Inspired by "Luke 5:1-11, the miraculous catch of fish", and Pope Saint John Paul II's use of the term "Duc in altum" ("into the deep"), from that passage and used as a phrase of impetus for the pastoral program for the third millennium, I took the name Altum Leadership Group. My motto, developed through the fifteen months of the Halftime roundtable, is "inspiring and equipping good leaders to become great."

It took over two years to "find my lane" and in this time I hardly earned any money. Annie and I had to cut back drastically on expenses, and whilst we always had enough to feed and educate you kids, there were no extras, and we struggled to make ends meet. My brother Dave was very generous, lending us money – three times – but it was sometimes hard to see a way forward for the business. At one point, I had $1.91 in the bank, and I remember trying to buy a coffee and having my card rejected! Jerome, at this point it dawned on you that things were tight indeed, and you said to me, "Gee dad, the business really isn't going well, is it?!"

Covid hit in March 2020, just at the time that the Lord had made it clear to me that my work was indeed to be within a faith context. Until this time I was unclear on this, thinking I was meant to serve in a "secular space," despite much of my work coming to me in the "faith space," even without marketing there. The next three months were cancelled or postponed, and I was forced to go on the Government's JobKeeper program, but for the second half of that year, while we were pretty much in lockdown the whole time, work started to come in. In the course of that time, a number of very good work arrangements were set up for the year that followed (2021, this year) and it truly seems like something extraordinary has happened. I literally feel that it is my equivalent of Jesus saying "put your net on the other side" after toiling fruitlessly all night, and then when doing so, the net is full of fish!

What was also amazing, however, is how even during the times of lean provisions God's care made it possible for me to take Annie to Europe for two weeks as a twenty-fifth wedding anniversary present. I recall how I had bought the flights and booked all the hotels etc. for the two weeks in France and Italy, and when I gave the gift at our anniversary Annie's face fell, as she was shocked, knowing we could not possibly afford it. I'd told her I had a way out, if need be, because the travel agent was holding them all till April, when I needed to confirm or cancel (our anniversary is December). In the very week we had to confirm or cancel, I had a lunch meeting with a leader of a law firm, David Wells, who asked me to coach one of his junior partners, Tony Rutherford, and to do so for the whole year, asking if, for tax purposes, he might pay me the whole sum upfront. I was blown away, partly because of the kind consideration of David (even though he genuinely believed the coaching would be of great service to Tony, which indeed it turned out to be), but also because it meant we could confirm the trip. After the meeting I immediately phoned Annie and told her, saying, "Do you agree that it seems God is wanting us to go on this second honeymoon?" to which she joyfully acquiesced, "Yes!" Learn about money, let it serve you, never let it be your master. Greed is a curse, and "the love of money is the source of all evil" (1 Tim 6:10), so if you can master it, let it be your servant, then the Lord will be generous in pouring it into your lap.

Some of the ways to master money, in my limited experience, and from what I have gleaned from those who are far more financially literate than me, include: put the money you earn first into primary needs, such as food and basic housing and daily living; don't spend money you don't have; avoid, wherever possible, getting into debt; don't be afraid of making investments, if sensible, and where these may require temporary debt, work to pay it off as quickly as possible; live simply, and make your financial goals correspond to your life goals; be totally honest in all your financial arrangements; pay people quickly when they provide goods or services; never undervalue yourself when you arrange contracts for work positions, or in the provision of goods and services in business deals. In short, be the master of money, let it serve you, don't serve it, but use it wisely, creatively and know that God is the Provider of abundance, so he will take care of you. Trust in Him.

The stories of both Job and Tobit, for example, show that hardship and impoverishment can come to virtuous and God-fearing men, and therefore one cannot presume an entitlement to wealth as a pay-off from God for faithfulness. God is neither a genie whose lamp we rub to force him to bow to our wishes, nor is he unmoved by our sufferings. He always seeks our greatest good, being Love Itself, and His mysterious ways are far from how we would do things. He may indeed call one or more of you to embrace, alongside the evangelical counsels of virginity for the Kingdom and obedience to a religious superior, the virtue of radical material poverty. And in this way, should you respond, you would be like Jesus himself who affirmed that "foxes have holes, and the birds of the air have nests, but the Son of Man has no place to rest his head" (Mt 8:20), and also, "blessed are you poor, for yours is the kingdom of God" (Lk 6:20).

In either case, whether you need wealth (to greater or lesser extent) or forsake wealth, God will always care for you. He will take care of your material and spiritual needs, and the focus on Saint Joseph in this year given to us by Pope Francis is a reminder of that. So, let us pray and trust and not worry:

> So I say to you: Ask, and it will be given to you; search and you will find; knock and the door will be open to you.
> For the one who asks always receives, the one who searches always finds, the one who knocks will always have the door opened to him.
> What father among you would hand his son a stone when he asked for bread?
> Or hand him a snake instead of a fish?
> Or hand him a scorpion if he asked for an egg?
> If you then, who are evil, know how to give your children what is good, how much more will the Heavenly Father give the Holy Spirit to those who ask him?!
> (Luke 11: 9-13).

Chapter Seventeen

Forgiveness

Please take note, my beloved sons, of the crucial – I choose this word "crucial" deliberately – role of forgiveness in your life. Forgiveness is the great unblocker! If you're blocked or lacking progress in your life, it may well be that you need to forgive yourself, or that you need to forgive someone. As we dare to pray in the "Our Father" prayer, "forgive us as we forgive others" (Mt 6:12). This chapter will outline three stories from my life – one relating to my childhood, another to my professional life as a footballer, and the third to my marriage – which I hope will illustrate its importance, the incredibly vital place of forgiveness.

On the 1st of January 1990 I went to a day run by the Catholic Charismatic Renewal in Melbourne, the focus of which was upon freedom through forgiveness. I went to a number of these things over those few years prior to, and including the early years after, the beginning of the Emmanuel Community in May of 1993. On one such occasion I asked to be prayed over by one of the prayer teams available, and in the prayer one of the women received an inspired message for me, which resounds to this day. She said, "it seems that the Lord is asking you to forgive your mother, and also to love her as she is, not to put conditions on your love." It struck me to the core!

In the years of fallout from the conflict between mum and dad and the separation, I desperately wanted them to be reunited. I was still grieving the loss of their foundational love, I was hurt by mum's departure from the Church, still recovering from the wounds of what I saw were the result of mum's antagonism towards dad, and I wanted mum to take steps to restore all of this, which hadn't happened. Without really realising it, I was judging mum and my heart was not free. I was making many efforts to love her but underlying them was a set of conditions that placed expectations upon her which I required her to meet. So, in fact, I was not loving her. She, of course, must have experienced all this, which meant there was a lack of freedom and genuineness in our relationship.

Therefore, the prophetic word I received to "forgive mum" and "love her as she is, without expectation," cut me to the heart and moved me to change. Over time, my attitude shifted, and I prayed for the grace to forgive her, and subsequently made many acts of forgiveness in my heart. I began to have a more compassionate perspective towards her actions of those years in my teens, opening my eyes, ears and heart towards the struggle she had to face: of moving to Australia with four young children with no extended family for support; to recognising the impact of the tragedy of her only sibling's – my uncle John's – horrific motorcycle accident in South Africa just after we departed there, leaving him with every bone in his body broken and a promising academic career in tatters; the limitations of dad's capacity to love her; and mum's projection onto dad of issues – I believe unresolved – relating to her own father's behaviour towards her mum and inside their family, all of which contributed to her nervous breakdown.

I could perceive that mum sensed a shift in my attitude, and since that time my relationship to mum has been really good. I think it has also helped mum's attitude towards me, as has Annie's total acceptance of mum and love for her and respect towards her. I am reminded of the exhortation of Saint Paul in his Letter to the Ephesians: "Do everything you can to preserve the unity of the Spirit by the peace that binds you together" (Eph 4:3).

My second forgiveness story took place when I was playing footy for Hawthorn. After the 1991 Premiership season, where I was Player of the Finals, I sustained a groin injury in the pre-season of 1992, which led to a series of groin and abdominal operations after dragging me down for a few seasons from 1992 to 1995. When Ken Judge came to Hawthorn as coach in 1996 it was clear that he saw no role for me in the team due to the recruitment of Paul Salmon from Essendon in what was an overt and public move to have him take the role of number one ruckman. It was very understandable, given Salmon's reputation, and was an entirely justified move, as Salmon became a great success at Hawthorn. It was Judge's treatment of me, his utter disdain for me, however, that was so hurtful. Even though Salmon was doing well, I still believed I had a place in the team, but for a number of weeks through the middle of 1996 I was not only in the Reserves, but not even playing well in the Reserves. By this time, it looked very likely that my career at Hawthorn was over.

At this time, I went to the Sacrament of Confession and, among other things, confessed that "I think I hate someone." I told the priest about the anger, frustration and hurt I felt in relation to my football coach, and my feelings of hatred towards what I believe was a direct malice held in relation to me from him. One thing that shifted within a short time after this Confession was my form. I began to play well in the Reserves. After a few matches of excellent form, I approached Judge and challenged him to pick me in the senior team. We had a confrontation that left me shaking, but which I think gave him a new respect for what he saw was a fighting spirit he had possibly not seen in me before. This may have been one of the graces of the whole episode, my need to fight and stand up for myself in the face of a person I experienced as a bully.

Before long I returned to the Senior team, playing in a new position in the back line, manning up on the tall forward – either a key marking player such as the Centre Half-Forward or the resting Ruckman in the Forward Pocket – and by season's end my form there warranted a new contract for the following year. My career had been saved, and 1997 saw me have a very good season in my rejuvenated career playing in defence. I played my final season in 1998, running out of steam as a 29-year-old, but it was a Confession at a low point in 1996, the forgiveness that came from it, and the fight which welled up within me because of it, that extended my career. This story has something of the episode of "Jacob wrestling with God" in it, the test which forces one to dig deeper and find something new to take up the challenge of life. I hope, beloved sons, that when you find yourself up against the wall, that forgiveness may be one of your primary options to help you find a way through.

My third forgiveness story is one that I often tell when speaking at men's conferences or events. And I usually begin by referring to beavers, those little American "critters" that create dams by gathering up many small sticks, and by piling them on top of each other to build a wall which blocks the flow of millions of litres of water down the river. I then explain that very rarely do relationships fall down as a result of one major action – though on occasion this may be true – but mostly it is by the accumulation of many small offences or neglect which build up and create an invisible wall between two people. I think we all know the experience of there being a distance that can emerge in relationships – whether personal or professional – where the other person, all of a sudden, seemingly inaccessible.

Such a time took place for me and Annie, my sons, a few years after we returned from Sydney to Melbourne, when you, Ambrose, were about five or six years old. There had been a period of a few months where I felt that your mum was quite distant from me, emotionally unattainable, that she had fallen into a kind of functional way of being, and certainly was not interested in being touched by me physically. This was new territory as we had never had such an icy period in our marriage. Despite what I felt were attempts from me to come close – in a variety of ways – I felt constantly, if subtly, rebuffed. That she was unwilling, clearly closed to, making love, was both hurtful and concerning, not only for its own sake, but also because it represented so much else.

One day I mustered the courage to speak frankly with her and said, "I don't feel that you cherish me anymore," to which she replied, "Well, I don't feel that I cherish you." At least she now stated it! I went on, "Why not? You've got to tell me." It had been one of those nights in bed, awkward, where Annie had been quietly sniffling, her back turned to me. When, on previous occasions, this had been the case we usually spoke things out, having, since the beginning of our marriage, lived according to the motto, "Don't let the sun go down on your anger." This practice has created a platform to ask forgiveness and seek it, and then to put the hurtful actions, words or neglect aside quickly and easily. Over the years we have been very good at doing this. I was probably the main pusher of this, being very sensitive to the potential impact of rifts in the relationship, having seen the outcome in my mum and dad's break up and conflict. Annie, on the other hand, comes from a very strong and unified family, her parents being both paragons of virtue and unified. The downside, however, of their strength, is that problematic issues aren't raised, which means at times things can stay beneath the surface. Annie has inherited this trait and over the years she has had to work to develop a more forthright approach to resolving conflict.

When I asked her to tell me what the problem is at this time she said, "there is something actually," and I said, "please tell me." As I have just mentioned she struggles to state outright when there is a problem, so I knew it was very important how I listened and received what she was about to say, and how I responded. "Well," she began, "when I was in labour with Ambrose you were on the phone a lot." My heart sank! I remembered well, it was 2006, and I was in full swing in my role as Director of Evangelisation and Catechesis for the World Youth Day that was to take place in 2008. The world was coming to Sydney and there were already huge things to deal with, but I knew she was right. I have always made a high priority of being present at the birth of all of you kids and have prided myself on how much presence and support I have provided to Annie in all of your labours, not letting anything get in the way of showing her my love and care while she was doing that most amazing and honourable service to life for each of you six kids. And yet, here she is pointing out how I failed with the last of you. I felt awful. I also knew that this was not a moment for explanation or justification. In fact, I had a very strong sense of the crucial nature of this moment and how I would react. So, I simply accepted as truth what she said, and repented: "I'm so sorry. You are right. I should have put my phone away and not allowed myself to get side-tracked while you were in labour. Can you forgive me?" She replied, thankfully, with: "I forgive you."

Over the years we have always tried to be clear with our language when asking for and giving forgiveness. "I'm sorry, I shouldn't have done that. It was wrong," or, "please forgive me, I didn't do (or say) that, when I should have." I have found it much easier to forgive when an act of sorrow is clear, up front and heartfelt, and which doesn't excuse oneself, qualify or skim over the problem. Sometimes there are mitigating factors, of course, such as pressure, tiredness or some other force. And these can be mentioned, if appropriate, but a good apology takes full responsibility for one's actions. Similarly, "I forgive you" is a clear and simple way of stating that it, whatever the offence, is now gone. Personally, I much prefer this to the vaguer "it doesn't matter" or "no problems," which don't necessarily acknowledge the wrong done or the need to ensure the action is not repeated. "I forgive you" does indeed include a recognition that "what you did was wrong but it is now gone."

After Annie forgave me (some five or six years after the offence, even though I had not been conscious of it, how embarrassing!), I asked her, "is there anything else?" She looked at me and said, rather sheepishly, "well, yes, there is, actually." And thus began the recounting of a series of offenses she outlined to me, one after the other, from the period of years, to which I simply said, "I'm so sorry, please forgive me." I felt like Rocky Balboa, taking a hiding of one blow after another, but was so pleased that Annie was freeing herself of these burdens that had so clearly been weighing on her. This conversation went for hours, and finally at about 2:30 a.m. in the morning I said, "Anything else?" "No, I think that is all," she replied. We were exhausted, there had been many tears, but the dam had now gone, and the river's waters flowed. We made love for the first time in months, and the intimacy and unity of it was better than ever before. What had seemed to be, only a few hours previously, a gulf of a million miles, was now gone, and our unity now seamless.

I'm fully aware that some marriage differences are irreconcilable, and that sometimes it is advisable for couples to remain apart, especially if there is danger or some such factor. However, I'm also a believer that what can appear to be major problems in a marriage may have a much quicker and simpler way forward than appears, but central to this is drawing deeply from the grace of the Sacrament of Marriage, requiring prayer, loving communication, and forgiveness. As the miracle of the Wedding Feast at Cana attests, the "best wine" comes from Jesus, who is Love Himself. So when couples "run out of wine," when it seems that they have no love left, they need to believe that, in fact, there is no shortage of love available to them. They need only find the ways to have access to that love unblocked, and that forgiveness, and the healing which accompanies it, is a primary means to bringing that unblocking about.

My beloved sons, practice forgiveness always. Be quick to say, "I'm sorry," be quick to say "I forgive you." May both be wholehearted. Make yourself available to the other, be sensitive to timing, allow for personal strengths, qualities and weaknesses when you seek to bring unity to fruition. Above all, pray for the grace to bring these to bear, for God is literally dying (and rising) to open these doors to us.

Chapter Eighteen
Gratitude

My beloved sons, I give thanks for each of you, the unique gifts, abilities, personality, and vocation of each, who you are, what you mean to me. No one is like you! My heart is filled with delight and wonder and joy, as I contemplate the masterpiece which each of you is, and which each of you is becoming, the Master Artist shaping you, adding a touch here, freshening the colour there.

This chapter is a focus on gratitude, as thanksgiving. It is both an acknowledgement of what is given, but also an act of trust that all *is* given, and thus opens up the possibility of new gifts. Gratitude is the disposition that is paired with generosity. When you know all is given, then you're not afraid to give. In fact, knowing that it "is in giving that we receive," a great person is not afraid to give. The person who holds tightly to his possessions, be they material or otherwise, is incapable of receiving more or better gifts. Even adversity can be a gift from God, because He can be stripping you of something in order to prepare the way for something better. All forms of negation serve that truth. It is why fasting, sacrifices, almsgiving, and the like, have value, even though in each case something which is good in itself is being forsaken. In times of trial or hardship, therefore, give thanks. In all things give thanks. Let "thank you" be constantly on your lips, and in your hearts.

I cannot move too quickly past my thanks for the gift of each of you. I wrote earlier of the miraculous announcement of your conception, Jerome, and to this day I marvel at it, and at you. Dom and Ambrose, in different ways, though no less dramatic, your pregnancies are also both notable. Dom, while inside your mum's womb, the ultrasound showed what might be a lack of a stomach, and the doctor, at a whim, suggested a "termination," which we rejected outright. When you were born, the beautiful and "perfect" (mum's joyful words) boy that you are, we gave thanks for you, and took great pleasure in presenting you to that doctor.

Needless to say, in the years since, we have seen no lack in that stomach of yours, a healthy appetite in which we rejoice. And for you, Ambrose, due to blood clots mum was required to take medication that led the doctor to tell her that you should not have been conceived, and that she should abort you. Again, we rejected this advice from the second doctor, but it meant mum changing the manner of taking the medications from oral to that of a daily self-administered injection into her upper leg. This is one example among many of your mum sacrificing for you! From the beginning, we have rejoiced that each of you is a gift, a unique, unrepeatable mystery to be marvelled at, but also defended, rejoiced in, nourished and blessed.

To all you men who are reading this, whether you are a husband to one of my daughters, a grandson, or a man who I have known and loved, or if you simply desire to receive something of what I have received and shared here, for all of you I give thanks. I am aware that, by God's grace, I have been called to provide fatherhood to many men, especially where in one way or another, it has been lacking, for no father is complete, me included. For drawing me into that wonderful mystery of somehow mediating God's fatherhood, albeit in a limited way, for we are but earthenware jars holding a priceless treasure, I give thanks.

Some people think giving thanks is a sign of weakness. I totally reject this idea as being based in pride. It comes from the same spirit which says, "I will not serve," that is, Lucifer.

The words "thank you" are signs of humility, if properly intended. Just as it is only a courageous man who can be a true gentleman, so too it is only one who is humble that considers acknowledging another person or their actions. A proud man won't listen to the advice of others, nor will he seek help, but a humble man knows his limitations and recognises the qualities of others. The humble man rejoices in the qualities of others and wishes to benefit from them as a "gift". This is what "thank you" means. It has at its essence a true "knowing" of the other, and the genuine charity to help them be "known".

I think we have all had the experience of being taken for granted, when we make an effort for someone and then, without any gratitude, they either ignore our efforts, or get what they want without thanking the person who gave it. This is a purely transactional way of behaviour; the person being forgotten. There is no love in this, it is simply using. An example from the Gospel jumps to my mind - when Jesus healed the ten lepers, only one returned to thank him. Nine made no acts of gratitude. They got what they wanted, ignored who gave it to them, and went on their way. How easy it is to be like that, not only with God whom we don't see, but even with people in our family, our friends, our colleagues, whomever, whom we do see.

It is no surprise then, considering how forgetful we can be, that God gives to us a constant reminder and built-in framework to give thanks to Him. This is called the Eucharist and it literally means "Thanksgiving." The Greek verb "*eucharistow*" translates into English as "to give thanks." In the Eucharist, where Jesus offers Himself to the Father for us as the "Lamb of God who takes away the sins of the world," he does so as a "memorial," that is, a sacred remembering of what he has done for us. He doesn't want us to forget! He wants us to give thanks - for Him and for each other!

To forget another person is the opposite of "Thanksgiving." When Pierre Goursat was nineteen years old he had an experience where he felt the presence of his brother who died some years earlier, and was admonished in that experience to the conviction that he had forgotten his brother. Somehow connected with this experience he received a deeper conversion to Jesus, and through these he eventually discovered his vocation to be a brother, a lay consecrated brother, and to realise this vocation within the Emmanuel Community which he helped to found. At the heart of the Emmanuel Community is what is called the Fraternity of Jesus - the brothers and sisters of Jesus. The grace of remembering was intricately intertwined with the realisation of the vocation of Pierre Goursat for himself personally and for the life and mission of the Emmanuel Community, the first priority of which is the Eucharist - in the Mass and in Eucharistic adoration.

To remember is also to be who we truly are. Annie often told me how, as a child but more specifically as a teenager and young adult, her dad would say to her or to her other siblings, "Now remember you are a Stewart!" This would often be said as a kind of exhortation to good behaviour, if, for example, they were on the way out for an evening. The key point for me, however, is the connection between memory and identity, and in that the power of simply knowing who you are as an antidote for searching for false promises. John Paul II spoke of this in relation to the Church in his work "Memory and Identity" in which, among other things, he sought to remind his readers how the Gospel came to Europe, and thus how the evangelisation of the West was realised. He did this in order to remind Europe of its origins in Christ, and to draw it out of the coma of forgetfulness into which it is falling (or, one could argue, has fallen). An individual who behaves badly might consider something similar, excusing himself of "being out of his mind," or "not himself," while pursuing illusory dreams that promise everything but deliver nothing, only misery. Let us always remember, therefore, all the good works of the Lord and give thanks.

I was recently struck by how the Gospel of Saint Luke starts with a fire, and in that sense parallels the Acts of the Apostles, which starts with the Pentecost fire. It is not surprising, given that St Luke wrote the Acts, too. But it had not occurred to me before that the Gospel of Luke, which begins in the Temple, zeroes in on the action of the fire at the altar of incense in the sanctuary itself. The priest Zachariah was attending to this fire when the angel of the Lord came to him with the news of the announcement of the coming birth of a son to him and his wife Elizabeth in their old age. This son, of course, was to be John the Baptist, the precursor to the Lord Jesus, the one who would prepare the Lord's coming, the one who would come in the spirit of Elijah, the prophet of fire. It is striking that this announcement takes place at the fire in the sanctuary of the Temple, at the very core place of worship for the people of Israel, and thus alludes to the fire at the heart of the locus of worship in the New Covenant, which we know to be the Temple which is the Body of Christ.

Jesus' Body replaced the Jewish Temple as the locus of worship for the People of God, through his death and resurrection and the institution of the Eucharist. For this reason, God allowed the destruction of the temple in 70 AD, an act of Roman aggression and domination to put down the Jewish uprising, and the Temple has never since been rebuilt. The fire in the sanctuary is an allusion to the Eucharistic fire which we are invited to receive when we partake in the offering of Jesus' Body and Blood.

This is the fire of the Holy Spirit, poured out into the world through the Church on the day of Pentecost, but continually made available to us who are Baptised into the Spirit, who are Confirmed in the Spirit, through our partaking in this Eucharistic fire.

As we see in the Resurrection story of the encounter of the two disciples on the road to Emmaus, it is a story of the fire of the Word of God – "were not our hearts burning within us as He spoke to us" (Lk 24:32) – and a fire of the Presence of God, for they recognised Him in the breaking of the bread. This fire gave the disciples new energy to return the seven miles to Jerusalem, to rejoin the community of believers, and to give testimony to what they had seen and heard, but also to hear the testimony of the others who had been inflamed in their turn. As Ephraim the Deacon said, "the one who eats the Eucharist with faith eats the fire of the Holy Spirit." This is not unlike in the call of Isaiah, upon whose lips the angel of the Lord put a coal from the fire of the sanctuary in heaven, a burning coal that purifies his lips but also puts the Lord's words on them. I feel it is also pointing us to the Eucharist, a flame from the sanctuary of the Body of the Lord, placed on the lips and indeed the tongue, to receive Jesus himself, to be inflamed by the Spirit, to worship and give thanks to God.

My sons, let this fire always live in you. Welcome it, prepare yourselves for it, tend it. Whether you are a husband, a father of a family, or one who is called to tend the fire of the Lord's sanctuary as Deacon, Bishop, or Priest in the spirit of Saints Stephen, Matthias or Barnabas, always, in all things, give thanks!

Chapter Nineteen

Greatness

Dear boys (even though you're all young men you will always be, in a certain sense, "my boys"), we now come to the concluding chapter of this book, *The Tiny Book for Giant Men*. Today is the feast day of the Birth of Saint John the Baptist, and it is a fitting day to conclude this writing, as he is one who in many ways exemplifies the apparent paradox at the heart of its title, the call to greatness through humility. He is the one, speaking of Jesus, who said, "He must increase, and I must decrease" (Jn 3:30). He is a very worthy model of manhood – self-sacrificial, prayerful, courageous, just, a voice of truth and moral uprightness, a witness to Jesus. Of him, Jesus Himself said, "There is no greater man born of woman than John the Baptist" (Mt 11:11). He is indeed "great" – a giant of a man!

I invite you to recognise your call to greatness, to the virtue of magnanimity, which is realised only with the virtue of humility. You are created for greatness, called to be a saint, and you will realise this purpose via humble surrender to God's grace and life in you, and through the service of others, according to your particular vocation and mission. Yes, you are limited, flawed, weak, a sinner! All of us are! Give the little you have, like the boy with only five loaves and two fish who, upon entrusting it to Jesus, saw them multiplied extraordinarily. However, you have also received so much, are gifted and talented in so many ways. Let your gifts, passions, interests and flair give glory to God! Do not be afraid!

We know that John the Baptist prepared the way for the Lord, but the way that prepared John the Baptist was paved when Mary, carrying Jesus in her body and, full of the Holy Spirit, visited Elizabeth. At Mary's greeting John the Baptist leapt for joy in his mother's womb and Elizabeth was filled with the Holy Spirit. So, it is Mary to whom I wish to draw your attention at the conclusion of this book, for she is the one whose "soul magnifies the Lord" (Lk 1:46), and therefore the one whom we go to in order to come closer to Him. She magnifies Jesus! She gives birth to Him and, as our mother, she gives birth to Jesus Christ in us. Let yourself be immersed in her, and she will best help you to become like Him. That is her vocation! She only ever says, "Do whatever he tells you" (Jn 2:5)!

As I have often told you, Annie and I, upon waking each morning, drowsily reach across the bed to find each other's hand, and our first words consist of the consecration to Mary of Saint Louis de Montfort, the simple version encouraged in the Emmanuel Community:

> Today we choose you Mary
> standing before all the saints,
> to be our mother and our Queen.
> We dedicate ourselves to you,
> in humility and love,
> our bodies and our souls,
> our gifts and our possessions,
> the merit of good deeds,
> those present, past and still come.
> We freely give you the right
> to deal with us, and everything we have
> as you see fit, for the greater glory of God,
> both now and for eternity. Amen.

This daily entrustment honours Jesus in His mother, for He gave her to us - with Saint John at the foot of the cross – to be our mother too! With Saint Joseph she raised Jesus to be a man, and she helped Joseph to be a man. No doubt she helped Peter and the Apostles to step into their manhood in ways they never would have without her. She shows the way that the feminine genius, to use Saint John Paul II's expression, is vital, alongside that of the qualities of good men, for the transition of good men to become great.

I recall a time in my late twenties, when there was an Emmanuel Community retreat in Melbourne, and we were very fortunate to have with us Martine and Herve Catta. Martine was, with Pierre Goursat, the co-founder of Emmanuel, a medical doctor who was very young at the time of the foundation of the community in the early 1970s. Herve, a lawyer, became her husband shortly after those days, and both of them were very spirit-filled evangelizers. Annie and I were in charge of the community in Melbourne, and I had been feeling flustered and out of my depth, trying to run the retreat. Seeing this, Martine, at a certain moment, put her hands on my shoulders, looked up at me with her sparkling eyes and joyful smile, and said, "You are a man!" Something very profound was strengthened in me with that affirmation, something wounded was healed, and something imprisoned was set free. I have never forgotten that moment or its impact! And it helps me to know that while it is certain and vital for men to become men through the presence, encouragement and fathering of other men, so too do men become men because of the women in their lives, the presence, empowerment and motherly love of women.

As I mentioned in the first chapter of this book, one of the reasons it is important for men to become who they really are is so that they can help women become who they really are. Similarly, it is just as true that it is needed for women to become who they truly have been created to be for many reasons including to help men become who they are created to be. The "battle of the sexes" leads to disaster, whereas the complementarity of the sexes is genius. The truth of the latter sits at the basis of all human fulfilment because the human capacity for love and communion, our essential relational qualities, are grounded in the communitarian nature of the one true God, who is Father, Son and Holy Spirit. This is partly why I will set out, after concluding the writing of this book, *The Tiny Book for Giant Men,* to write a book for your sisters and for women who may be interested, which will be called *The Tiny Book for Beautiful Women.*

Anybody who knows you boys is well aware of how aptly titled this book is, for all of you physical sons of mine stand over 190cm. Even you Ambrose, though still only fifteen years old, are already a physical giant. More significantly, however, all men, whether tall, short or in between, are called to be giant in the stature of their souls and their character. John Paul II said that every boy must be told he can do it! This book is attempting to do that for you. Similarly, John Paul II said that every girl must know she is beautiful! Your three sisters are – like their mother – very beautiful women, as all who know them can attest, strikingly beautiful indeed! More significantly, however, is that their beauty shines gloriously through their virtue and their spirits, as with all women, even if they do not model clothing or don the cover of Vogue magazine.

On that note, then, allow me to conclude this book by giving praise, thanks and honour to God for the gift of Annie, your mum, most certainly the greatest created gift I have received, my best friend, my lover, my closest companion, my soul mate, my way of holiness. And let me do so by quoting some lines from the Book of Proverbs, which begin, "A perfect wife - who can find her?" Whenever this is read in Mass, especially when I'm with Annie, I put my hand up a little, lean over and whisper into her ear, "I've found her!":

> A perfect wife - who can find her?
> She is far beyond the price of pearls.
> Her husband's heart has confidence in her,
> from her he will derive no little profit...
> Advantage and not hurt she brings him
> all the days of her life... (Prov 31:10-12).

My dear sons – Dom, Jerome, and Ambrose, and all my sons – I have concluded this book with a chapter that features Mary. It is her capacity, the grace given to her, which leads us as men into our call to holiness as men. As part of this, she points us to Joseph, the man God chose to be the human father of Jesus, who in a real sense is our father, to guide us as men of God. In this Year of Saint Joseph, the 150th anniversary of the promulgation of Saint Joseph as the Patron of the Universal Church, the Holy Spirit is leading us more deliberately to him who taught Jesus how to be a man, so as to teach each of us how to be a man. Joseph is truly a giant of a man, a giant among men!

Listening to, and responding to, the Word of God, therefore, which exhorts us to "Go to Joseph" (Gen 41:55), let us also consecrate ourselves as men to his fatherly heart, his chaste heart, so that, together in the love of the Immaculate Heart of Mary – whose triumph we pray for and await – we may dwell deeply within the tender, merciful and burning Heart of Jesus, whose heart is the Heart of God.

My sons, I love you, I cherish you, I believe in you!

With these words, I now finish this tiny book for you, and for men who would read it, and through it I hope that all of you become, more and more, giant men.

www.ingramcontent.com/pod-product-compliance
Lightning Source LLC
Chambersburg PA
CBHW020144130526
44591CB00030B/206